the Property Makeover Price Guide:

Organising & Budgeting for Home Improvers & Developers

'The next time a tradesman looks at your drains, gutters or re-decorating job, sucks hard between his teeth and delivers an eye-watering estimate, reach for this empowering new book'.

www.expressandstar.com

'If one of your new year's resolutions is to finally sort out some long put-off repairs on your house, the Property Makeover Price Guide will be a must have addition to your toolbox'

Liverpool Daily Post

The Building Cost Information Service

The Property Makeover Price Guide:
Organising & Budgeting for Home Improvers & Developers

© BCIS 2007

ISBN 978 1 904829 52 2

BCIS
12 Great George Street
Parliament Square
London SW1P 3AD

www.bcis.co.uk

BCIS is a trading name of RICS

Printed in Wales by Print Direction Ltd, Llanmaes, Wales www.printdirection.co.uk
Designed by Yogi Creative Ltd, Cardiff, Wales www.yogicreative.co.uk

the Property Makeover Price Guide

Contents

Part 1

1.1 Introduction

1.2 Cost Information

1.3 Employing a Contractor

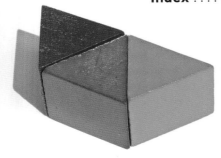

PART ONE

1.1 INTRODUCTION

Introduction

This guide will help you if you want to:

- Do up a property and sell it
- Improve your own home
- Fix a problem with your home

There are lots of books available telling you what to do to improve your property. What they don't usually tell you is what it will really cost. This guide does.

The guide:

- Gives you the cost information that will enable you to budget for repair, improvement, alteration and extension work, and
- Walks you through how to obtain builders or specialist contractors to actually do the work.

A Cautionary Tale

If you've watched any of the TV home makeover and property development programmes you'll know that it is very important to get your budget right before starting any construction project.

Some of the TV makeover programmes only talk about the costs of materials. If you were to run some of these projects yourself, you would need to budget the cost of all those workmen 'the labour' and what it would cost you to get advice from the 'TV experts'.

On the development programmes, the budgets set by the participants are often too low.

- The cost of good design work is underestimated.
- They expect a higher quality than their budgets will allow.
- Generally, they are over optimistic about what you can get for your money.

Repairs – 'a stitch in time saves nine'

With repairs, the stitch in time saying certainly applies. The main rule in looking after a property is to ensure that you carry out repairs before small defects lead to serious problems and therefore major costs.

When doing up a property for sale it is important that you get the basics right before upgrading the decorations and fittings. Or, in other words, there is no point putting in a new bathroom if the roof is dodgy and will leak in the first heavy rain of winter.

The guide gives you advice on

- The types of work you may need to undertake when doing up a property, together with approximate costs.
- An idea of the costs for alteration and repair work.
- Costs for a range of new extensions, porches, conservatories, garden rooms and garages.

There is also guidance on:

- Selecting contractors.
- How to carry out the work.
- Deciding payment - what to pay, to whom and when.
- Changing your mind - what to do if you want to ask for something different to be carried out - variations and extras.

There are common pitfalls in all these areas and this guide will help keep you out of trouble.

You may be able to get grants from your local authority for renovation work. This guide explains the eligibility, the limits and how to apply them. It is worth a look but the reality is that unless you are on a low income, you are unlikely to be eligible.

Layout of the Guide

This guide is in four parts:

Part One

- Introduction
- Layout of the guide
- How to use the guide
- Major property problems
- Extensions and alterations to the property
- How to employ a contractor
- Planning and building legislation and regulations to consider before undertaking the work, particularly with regards to works of alteration and new works
- Party walls, building materials and grants.

Part Two

The main part of the guide contains the cost information on items of repair, alterations, and new works.

- Items of Repair
  - o Work to the fabric of the property
  - o Services
  - o Finishes
  - o Redecoration
- Common alteration work
  - o Reroofing the property
  - o Forming openings within the building
  - o Retiling walls
  - o Replacing flooring
  - o Replacing doors and fireplaces
  - o Replacing sanitary suites and heating systems
  - o New drain runs and manholes.
- New works - total project costs
  - o New extensions
  - o Conservatories
  - o Garden rooms
  - o Loft and basement conversions
  - o New porches
  - o Garages and car ports

  - o Kitchen replacement
  - o Bathroom replacement.

Part Three

- Costing assumptions used in build up of the prices in this guide
- General building information
- Useful contacts.

Glossary

The glossary will help you talk to the builder. The cost information is described in terms that a builder understands. Of course this means that there will be some items where you may say 'well what on earth is that'. The glossary will help you to get around this problem.

How to Use the Guide

For any building project you should follow some simple steps:

1. Identify the work required.
2. Consult specialists where appropriate.
3. Produce a budget.
4. Consult a contractor(s).
5. Adjust your budget for any additional work identified.
6. Obtain quotes.
7. Agree payment schedule.
8. Commence work.

Part 1.2 of the guide shows how the information has been presented and suggests how it can be used.

It is important that you read the Introduction in full before trying to use the costs in this guide on a specific project of repair, alteration or extension work.

1.2 COST INFORMATION

About the Cost Information
The cost information in Part Two is in six sections.

1. Repairs
This covers most of the items of repair work that you will need to do to the existing fabric of the property.

They have been identified as defects:
- eg 'window is damaged or rotten'

With a solution:
- eg 'replace window'

And guide prices for various types and sizes of window
- eg timber casement window 600 x 900mm - £445

The cost will apply equally if you decide to replace the windows for aesthetic rather than practical reasons ie you just don't like them.

2. Services
This section includes all repair work to water, electricity and heating installations.

3. Finishes
This section provides costs for repairing and replacing floor, wall and ceiling finishes within the property.

4. Redecorations
This provides prices for repainting walls, ceilings, doors, windows and woodwork.

5. Common alterations works and indicative costs
These cover work you may do to change the way a property works eg forming openings, or installing false ceilings, replacing the heating system, or a bathroom suite.

6. Total project costs
This section provides prices for extensions, conservatories, etc and for replacing a kitchen or bathroom including fittings and equipment.

What is Included in the Costs
The costs given in all the tables include for everything necessary to carry out the works. This includes:
- Labour
- Material
- Contractors' overheads and profit
- Scaffolding and plant required to carry out the work
- Value Added Tax.

For small items of work the costs have also included the contractors call out charge (see Page 10).

House Sizes
Where the cost is for work to a whole house, two examples are given to indicate the range of likely costs:
- Terraced. A terraced house of 21m^2 area on plan (42m^2 total on two floors).
- Detached. This refers to a detached house of 125m^2 on plan (250m^2 on two floors).
  Elevation drawings of the houses used are included in Part Three.

Call out Charges
Contractors will often charge you for coming to your house. This is referred to as a 'Call out charge'. For small items of work the call out charge may be more than the cost of carrying out the work. Some contractors will include the first half hour of any work in the call out charge, this is particularly common with 'emergency' services such as drain clearing.

Generally, call out charges have been included in items under £250.

BCIS carried out a survey of contractors' call out charges for this book. Call out charges differ between, and within, the trades. Call out charges for a general builder ranged from £15 to £80, plumbers £25 to £55, roofers £45 to £350 and electricians £20 to £80. The costs included in the rates given in the guide are:

- General builder, carpenter, plumber, plasterer, glazier, painter   £50
- Roofer   £175
- Electrician   £35

Where more than one item of work is carried out on a single visit only one call out charge will apply and you should adjust the costs in the guide accordingly. An example of this adjustment is shown on Page 13.

Where a contractor has quoted for work the call out charges should be included in his quote.

The Cost Tables

Choosing the costs: The tables shows costs for items of works. Against each item, costs are given for a range of quantities.

In the example below, costs for hanging wallpaper are given for a wall of average height and various lengths. The area of wall is also given in m^2.

Description

Walls 2.75m high

Length	3m m^2 8	4m m^2 11	5m m^2 14	8m m^2 22
Repaper walls	**£**	**£**	**£**	**£**
Hang woodchip or embossed paper	155	190	230	335
Hang woodchip or embossed paper and decorate	220	280	345	450
Hang vinyl paper (PC £8 per roll)	235	315	370	490

Using the Costs from the Tables

Adjusting for quantity. The costs given are for a range of quantities eg. in the above example, for 8, 11, 14 and 22m2 of wall. You may need to adjust these for different quantities. This can be done in two ways.

Applying a unit rate. You can calculate a unit rate cost/m2 in this example and apply it to the required quantity.
Eg. Hanging 25m2 of woodchip paper:

22m2 costs:	£335
1m2 costs:	$\frac{£335}{22} = £15/m2$
25m2 costs:	**£15/m^2 x 25/m^2**
	= £375

Note that if you do the same calculation using the cost of 14m^2 this estimates the cost of hanging 25m^2 of woodchip paper at £410.

Pro-ratering. Alternatively, for some items where the range of costs is large you may wish to pro rata the costs

between the quantities.
Eg. Hanging 10m² of woodchip paper:

$$11m^2 \text{ costs: } £190$$
$$8m^2 \text{ costs: } £155$$
3 additional m² costs: £190-£155
$$=£35$$
1 additional m² costs: $\dfrac{£35}{3}$ = £12
2 additional m² costs: £12 x 2 = £24

10m2costs: £155+24   = £179

If the quantity of work is beyond the scope of the quantities given in a table an estimate can be made, within reason, by extrapolation. For example:
Eg. Hanging 25m² of woodchip paper:

$$22m^2 \text{ costs: } £335$$
$$14m^2 \text{ costs: } £230$$
8 additional m² costs: £335-£230=£105
1 additional m² costs: $\dfrac{£105}{8}$ = £13
3 additional m² costs: £13 x 3 = £39
25m² costs: £335+39 = £374

Adjusting for Location

The cost of building work varies around the country.

The costs in this guide represent UK 'national average costs'. They may need to be adjusted for location, and adjustment factors are provided in Section 3.3.

- If the total cost of the project is less than £1,000 then it is probably not worth adjusting for location.
- For projects likely to cost more than £1,000 it would be worth your thinking about the affect of location.

Using the Location Factors

The costs from the tables should be multiplied by the factors for the area where the project is located:

For example, costs in Wales are generally lower than the national average. The location factor for Wales is 0.91. Therefore, a project calculated to cost £100,000 from the table, is likely to cost £100,000 x 0.91 if it is located in Wales = £91,000.

Similarly, it is generally more expensive to build in Greater London. The location factor for London is 1.12. Therefore, a project calculated to cost £100,000 from the table, is likely to cost £100,000 x 1.12 if it is located in London = £112,000.

These adjustment factors relate to the cost of doing work and not the specification of the work. So adjusting the cost of installing a bathroom to London prices allows for the additional cost of fitting out a bathroom of a given standard, it does not allow for the difference in specification that might be appropriate in the different locations eg. between a B+Q bathroom and a Czech & Speake bathroom.

The location factors also allow comparison of costs between regions. If you know the cost of replacing a bathroom in Wales then you can work out what it might cost in London, as follows:

Known cost of our
bathroom in Wales **=£10,000**
Location factor for Wales = 0.91
Location factor for
Greater London = 1.12
Difference in price between
Wales and Greater London = $\dfrac{1.12}{0.91}$ = 1.23

Estimated cost of our
bathroom in Greater
London = £10,000 x 1.23 = **£12,300**

Rounding

The costs in the tables have been rounded to reflect the nature of the guide. Generally costs have been rounded as follows:

- Less than £100 rounded up to the nearest £1 eg. £51.49 has been shown as £52.
- From £100 to £1000 rounded up to the nearest £5 eg. £846 has been shown as £850.
- Greater than £1000 rounded up to the nearest £10 eg. £1447 has been shown as £1450.

These rounding conventions are not intended to imply a level of predictive accuracy.

Cost Base and Inflation

The costs in the tables are current at 4th quarter 2005. Adjustments for future inflation can be found in Part Three, where forecasts of costs over the next three years are shown.

Costing Assumptions and Procurement Context

Costs in this guide are for completing the work described as an individual job. They include contractors' overheads, scaffolding, where applicable, and VAT. They exclude any temporary works, contingencies and any fees that may be applicable. Details of these items are described in Part Three.

Building costs are influenced by a range of factors such as:

- Quantity of work
- When work is carried out
- Availability of space to work and store materials
- Provision of water and power
- The need for scaffolding
- Availability of materials and labour

These factors are the context in which you procure the work.

The costs in this guide are based on the assumptions about the procurement context that are given in the Costing Assumption in Part Three together with advice on how they influence costs. You should be aware of these assumptions and adjust the costs where actual circumstances differ.

There is no 'right' cost for building work. It is always an agreed price between a willing seller - the contractor, and a willing buyer - you. When there are shortages of labour prices will rise, when there is a shortage of work they will go down. In recent years, there has been a shortage of labour, an acute shortage in some areas, but the influx of builders from the new EU member states has helped to ease that situation.

The costs in this guide are intended to be reasonable where there is a sufficient supply of labour.

Costing Repairs – Examples
Example A

Property – 4 bedroom detached house. Gutter to front elevation is overflowing and two gutter joints are leaking due to blockage.

From Part 2 - Repairs - Exterior
Page 41
Clean out gutters
and outlets   £155
Page 41
Apply mastic sealant to
2 No. gutter joints @ £36   £72
                                     £227

Omit contractors
callout charge   £-50
(The two charges included above
therefore reduce to one charge)
Total Cost of Works   **£177**
                                       say   **£200**

Example B
Property – 3 bedroom semi detached
house. Insulation to roof space is
100mm thick and in very poor condition.

From Part 2.1 - Repairs - Insulation
Page 69
Clear out insulation and vacuum
roof space and lay 250mm thick glass
fibre insulation Area of roof space 42m².
Range:
Terraced House 21m² roof area £525
Detached House 125m2 roof area £3130

Unit cost £525 ÷ 21 =   £25/m²
Cost of example
42m² @ £25/m² =   £1050
Total Cost of Works   **£1050**
                             say   **£1100**

Example C
Property: Any
Refurbish room size 3 x 3m on first
floor, replace two rotten floor joists and
badly damaged ceiling; redecorate
throughout and replace skirting and
carpet.

Replace joists and ceiling
From Part 2.1 Repairs
Page 74
Replace 50 x 150mm floor joist
Take up floor boards,
renew joists, refix boards
      3m long joists 2 No @ £170   £340

From Part 2.3 Finishes
Page 127
Replace ceiling
Replace plasterboard ceiling
and emulsion paint
      Room 3 x 3 1 No @ £380   £380

From Part 2.4 Redecorations
Page 145
Clean and redecorate door and
frame (without fanlight) one side
      1 No @ £110   £110
Page 150
Clean and decorate window,
with two panes,
size 1500 x 1200mm
      1 No @ £81   £81
Page 143
Redecorate plaster walls
with emulsion paint   £265

From Part 2.3 Finishes
Page 129
Replace and decorate skirting
      Room 3 x 3 1 No @ £275   £275
Page 128
Replace carpet and underlay   £605
                                      £2,056

Omit contractors call out charge
(Four charges included above, remove
all as no call out charge required)
builders call out charge
      4 No @ £50   £-200

Total Cost of Works   **£1856**
                          say   **£1900**

1.3 EMPLOYING A CONTRACTOR

When do I use a Contractor?

If you are not a DIY person then you will want to employ a contractor for everything. Even if you are DIY person there are some tasks that it will be prudent to ask a general builder or specialist tradesman to undertake.

Note: Most electrical and all gas work is required to be carried out by a suitably qualified tradesman.

It will always be more economical to 'bundle' work together so if there are several items of repair that need to be done, and you can afford it, then these can be included together into one contract.

When should I Consult a Surveyor or Engineer?

For most items of repair and redecorations, contractors can offer all the advice on specification that you will need. However, on larger projects or where there are major structural works or a high level of design is required, you should consider using the services of a surveyor, engineer or architect.

Finding a Surveyor, Engineer or Architect

There are again several ways of finding a local surveyor, architect or engineer although the best method is to contact the various Institutions, such as The Royal Institution of Chartered Surveyors, The Royal Institute of British Architects, and The Institution of Structural Engineers. The details of these organisations are to be found in Part Three.

Finding a Contractor

A Contractor may be found from a variety of sources:

- Word of mouth from family, friends and neighbours.
- Nameboards outside other properties where work is in progress.
- Contacting the Local Authority.
- Contacting local architects and surveying practices.
- Contacting the Federation of Master Builders to obtain a list of local contractors.
- Advertisements in local newspapers.
- Yellow Pages and Thomsons' telephone directories.
- Internet search.

Selecting a Contractor

It is absolutely essential that you get the right contractor to carry out the work.

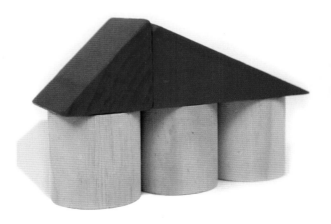

Selection of the appropriate contractor/tradesman

Choose a contractor who has experience of doing the type of work that you need doing. If only one type of work is required, then it may be better to select a tradesman, such as a plumber, rather than a general builder.

For example, employ a roofer for roof work rather than a general contractor

If several different types of work are needed then it is usually correct to select the trade whose work makes up the largest proportion of the whole, however, some trades may not be prepared to act as main contractor.

For example:
Replacing a bathroom suite – select a plumber.

Refurbishing a bathroom complete with new suite, tiles, flooring, shelving, cupboards, lighting and redecoration – select a general builder who can supervise all trades he cannot undertake.

Choosing a contractor

You must select the contractor very carefully. While there may be a very large number of local builders, be as selective as possible in order to prevent any future problems both with the works and finances. The larger the project the more important this becomes.

In your search for a contractor, BCIS recommends the following sequence:

- Family and friends - Obtain recommendations from family and friends, in the area, who have had similar work undertaken.
- Recommendation - Speak to neighbours to ascertain if a contractor has been recommended by word of mouth.
- Nameboards – when driving around the area look for nameboards on properties where work is being carried out.
- Local Authority - contact the local planning/building inspection department and ask if they have a list of recommended contractors.
- Local architects/local surveyors - contact to see if they can recommend any companies.
- Letting Agencies – will usually rely on a small group of contractors to carry out repair work at tenancies they manage. They may be prepared to share their contacts with you.
- Builders Federations - Contact your local builders' association and ask for a list of registered members. The National Federation of Builders has 14 offices around the country, which can provide lists of registered builders in your area. This can similarly be undertaken

for specific tradesmen eg. electricians.

When several names have been collected, contact the companies and ask if you:
- Can inspect current/past work. (**Visit** the work, inspect the quality and speak to owners about the performance and standards of the contractor)
- Obtain references. (**Check** the references)
- Does the builder belong to a respected trade body? (**Call** body to confirm membership is current)

Discuss with the contractors/tradesman the work to be undertaken and confirm with them whether and when they will be able to carry out the works.

Where the works are of a substantial nature, the choice of a contractor may be limited to the larger size contractors in the area. Discussions with the contractor and examination of his present and immediate past schemes will reveal his suitability to the works required.

Large contractors sometimes have small works departments who are capable of carrying out minor repairs, however these may charge more as they will have higher overheads (office staff etc) than those of a small builder.

Preparing a Budget for the Works

When putting together a budget for larger projects, it is important that the budget is an estimate of the cost of the work, not an estimate of how much you have to spend.

Once you have prepared the budget for the work, you need to decide if you can afford it. This is particularly important if you are acting as a developer. Too many first time investors in property see the budget as the remainder of sale price less the cost of the property, selling and buying costs and desired profit.

A proper budget sets the price you are prepared to pay for the property, not the budget for the required building work.

For example:

Potential sale price of property when renovated	£350,000
Buying and selling costs	£20,000
Required building work	£75,000
Finance charges	£27,000
Required profit	£30,000
Other costs	£5,000
=	£157,000

Value of property to developer **£193,000**

The budget should itemise all the required work and allow a contingency for unforeseen costs. The size of the contingency will depend on how sure you are of what you want and the level of alterations work that may uncover requirements for further work.

A contingency of 5% may be appropriate for a fully designed new extension, while 20% may be more appropriate if you are making major alterations to an old property.

Remember, this is your contingency budget, not the builders!

Estimates and Quotations

Before seeking estimates, make sure that you gather together as much information about the work as possible.

Select the appropriate materials. The cheapest are not necessarily the best, especially with regards to duration and future replacement.

Obtain information from manufacturers/installers as they will advise on the appropriate solution to a problem.

Allow a sum (possibly 10%) for contingency for hidden work or extra work that may arise during the contract. Builders may discover things that need fixing as jobs progress.

Obtain three quotes from contractors/tradesmen including the date that they will be able to commence the work. Ensure that the cost quoted will be fixed to the date they can undertake the work.

Request breakdowns of the quotes to examine and compare prices. A breakdown will also be extremely useful should variations and additional works be needed.

Contracts

A simple contract is a written **offer** to carry out the works for an amount and a written **acceptance** of that offer.

A simple but clear contract should be prepared for small contractors. However, for large contractors a formal contract using the Joint Contracts Tribunal (JCT) Minor Works Contract may be more appropriate.

Items that should be incorporated into a contract using small contractors/tradesmen should include:

- The cost of the work detailed on the drawing(s)/specification.
- The period of time the work is to be carried out in.
- Client requirements such as the contractor's access to the working area, any limitations on storage of

his materials and plant, and any protection required for other areas of the property during the execution of the works.

- The percentage of retention to be held by the client, and at what stage it will be released.
- The payment periods and calculation.
- Space for signature and dating by both parties.

Whilst the JCT contract is far safer both for the client and the contractor, for small builders this may be too onerous and they may be reluctant to price work that includes such a contract. Where the works are of a substantial nature, the employment of a professional surveyor, architect etc, is recommended. They will recommend the form of contract to use and prepare the documentation

Payments

On small contracts, where work may be expected to be completed in a few days, you should agree to pay the contractor on completion. Cash flow is always a problem for small businesses, and builders are no exception, so once you are happy with the work, but only when you are happy, pay promptly.

Never pay in advance. It is almost impossible to recover money overpaid without recourse to expensive legal action. If a contractor asks for payment for materials, agree either to pay the supplier directly or on delivery.

On larger projects the payment periods and calculation should be specified in the contract.

For example:
'Valuations shall take place on a fortnightly basis and shall be valued on the work completed by that date. Payment shall be made to the contractor within seven days of the valuation.'

Do not pay early for work and especially, do not overpay early.

Include the adjustment for retention with each payment

The calculation of how much is owing to a contractor is called a 'Valuation'.

An example of a valuation is set out as follows;

Value of total scheme including variations £53,000

Valuation No. 3

Value of work undertaken to date	£36,000
Variations No.1 and 2 completed	£2,000
Total of work completed	£38,000
Less retention @ 5%	£1,900
Total less retention	£36,100
Less Valuations 1 and 2	**£28,400**
Total	**£7,700**
Value Added Tax @ 17.5%	£1,348
Total due to contractor – Valuation No.3	**£9,048**

On completion of the works, carry out an inspection with the contractor and agree where any items have not been finished.

For example:
A new door is fitted including new ironmongery and decoration but the door does not close and on inspection requires planing on one side and subsequently redecorating.

Once the works have been fully completed, the retention can then be released.

Retention

This is a sum of money set aside by the client [you] from the contract sum until the works are completed to your satisfaction.

The inclusion of retention gives you some financial leverage and safeguard should some items of work, albeit minor, not be completed to your satisfaction. The money withheld will not be released until all the works are completed satisfactorily.

Should the contractor leave the site and not return to complete the outstanding works, you will have funds available to

have the work completed by others. You should notify the contractor if you are going to do this.

The details of the retention requirement should be set out in the original contract. It is usual to express retention as a percentage of the cost of the work, 5% being an appropriate and usual percentage.

Any variations should be included in the adjustment for retention.

As the works progress and payments are made, so the retention should be included with the payment calculations, see example under payments.

Variations and Extras

Always try to avoid changing your mind about what you want. However, even on the best run schemes 'stuff' happens, so changes are required.

Always obtain prices before agreeing for additional works to be undertaken, and confirm the work and cost in writing. Consult with the contractor as early as possible on possible variations, and ensure variations do not arise on work that has already been completed.

It may be a good idea to include additional works to an existing contract, rather than carry out this work at a later date as a separate job.

For example:
Existing job – replacing bathroom suite, retiling two walls to half room height, redecorating room.

Additional work; tile all walls to full height.

If the tiling hasn't commenced and the tiles are readily available then it should be cheaper and will be less disruptive if the work is added into this contract.

Keep variations and extra work to a minimum. If there are too many variations or even one variation of large importance/size then this may have an adverse effect on the contract completion date and therefore could increase costs.

When contracts of repair and refurbishment are undertaken, extra work may arise from hidden unforeseen problems.

For example:
Existing job – replacing ceiling.
On removal of the ceiling, the joists are found to be rotten and require replacing.

It may be prudent to allow a larger contingency sum in the budget for such works, to cover for any unforeseen or additional works.

1.4 PLANNING AND BUILDING LEGISLATION AND REGULATIONS

Introduction

If you are altering or extending your property there are two kinds of approval that you may require from your local authority.

- Planning permission – this is approval to increase the amount of building, so relates generally to extensions or outbuildings.

- Building Regulations – this is approval that building work is being carried out in accordance with the current Building Regulations. It relates to all new work and all structural alterations.

Planning Permission

Planning permission is the responsibility of the Local Authority.

It is permission to erect or extend a building.

Before commencing work on the design, it is generally a good idea to contact the Local Authority planning officer to seek their requirements and advice. The level of informal advice that you get depends very much on the individual planning officer.

For formal planning permission, the Authority will normally charge a fee. You [the applicant] will be required to submit your application using forms obtainable from the Authority.

Should you do the work without the necessary approvals, the Local Authority can issue an enforcement notice. This notice might require that you seek retrospective planning permission approval. However, there is no guarantee that retrospective permission will be granted. The Local Authority may even require that the completed work be demolished.

Listed buildings and properties in a conservation area have special planning requirements. Similarly, flats also have special planning requirements. It is again recommended that the Local Authority planning officer is consulted as early as possible on these types of properties.

Extensions

Planning permission for a single or two storey structure will depend on the floor area/volume in relation to the existing property.

Planning permission is required:
- In England and Wales, if the total addition to the original house is more than 70m³ or 15% of the volume of the original house, up to a maximum of 115m³, whichever is the greater. For a terraced house or property in a conservation area this

is $50m^3$ or 10%. In Scotland, if the total addition to the original house is more than 50m3 or one fifth of the volume of the original house, up to 115m3, whichever is the greater. If the house has been extended before, this must be added to the new work and together this must be less than the limit.

- When the extension is within 20m of the highway. If, however, the original house is less than 20m from the highway, the proposed extension must not be nearer to the highway than the original house.
- Any part of any extension, within 2m of the boundary, is more than 4m high.
- The extension projects above the highest part of the original house.
- The total area of the extension exceeds half of the garden area.

Note: Measurements are taken around the outside of the house.

Conservatories
The rules for conservatories will be the same as for single storey structures, above.

Porches
Planning permission is required for porches if:

- The floor area exceeds 3m2.
- Part of the porch is higher than 3m above ground.
- Part of the porch is less than 2m from the boundary between the garden and the public footpath/road.

Garages and car ports
If the garage is located within 5m of the original building, it will be considered as an extension and the same rules apply.

If the garage is situated more than 5m from the original building, planning permission is required if:

- The floor area is more than $15m^2$.
- The height is more than 3m high for a flat roof or 4m high for a pitched roof.
- There is sleeping accommodation.
- The garage covers more than half the area of the garden (excluding the area covered by the house).
- Part is less than 1m from a boundary.
- Part projects beyond any wall of the property facing the road.
- Use is only for anyone other than the house occupants.

Loft conversions
Loft conversions are subject to the same rules as extensions.

The volume to be considered will be only the additional volume outside the existing roof, eg. the volume created if a new dormer window is to be installed. In most cases, therefore, the increase in volume will be small.

Walls, fences and gates
Planning permission is required if walls, fences and gates are higher than 2m, or if they adjoin a highway they must be higher than 1m.

Building Regulations
Building Regulation approval is the responsibility of the Local Authority.

These Regulations define how the new building is to be constructed and ensure that the building is structurally safe, and that:

- New or existing foundations are adequate for the new construction.
- Rainwater and drainage conform to requirements.
- Staircases etc meet safety requirements.
- Ventilation, thermal insulation and fire safety regulations are complied with.

It is recommended that, before commencing work on the design, you contact the Local Authority building control officer to seek their requirements and advice.

The Authority will normally charge a fee and the applicant will be required to submit his application using forms obtainable from the Authority. A fee will also be charged for the visits by the building inspector.

The local building inspector will visit the site at specified stages in its construction in order to inspect the work. The building inspector may change requirements following his inspection, if he deems them necessary. For example, one of his first inspections will be carried out after the foundation trenches have been excavated. He will be in a position to examine the subsoil, and if not of a requisite standard, he could instruct that the depth of foundation be increased before the concrete is poured.

Structural alterations to existing building

All structural alterations such as forming openings, removing walls, removing chimney breasts etc, require Building Regulation approval. If you are not sure what is and what is not structural, consult the Local Authority, a surveyor or engineer.

Single or two storey structures built onto the existing building

Building Regulations approval is required where the extensions contain habitable rooms.

Conservatories

The definition of a conservatory is a building, which is attached to a building. It has more than 75% of the roof areas and more than 50% of the wall areas as translucent materials.
Building Regulations approval is required:
- When floor area exceeds 30m^2.
- When the conservatory is classified as a habitable room.

Porches

Building Regulations approval is required:

- When floor area exceeds 30m2.

Garages and car ports

Building Regulations approval is required:

- If the garage adjoins the house.
- If the garage is detached, and
    - When floor area exceeds 30m².
    - It is not more than 1 metre from a boundary or
    - It is more than single storey height, and
    - It is not constructed wholly of non-combustible material.
    - There is sleeping accommodation.
- If the car port is:
    - Not open on at least two sides, and
    - When floor area exceeds 30m².

Loft conversions

Building Regulations approval is required.

The structural requirements for any extension will apply here. The existing loft may create problems with regards to both headroom and the size of the existing floor joists.

If the loft is created on a third or higher floor then there must be an adequate means of fire escape. Possible solutions include:

- Enclosing the stairway and landing with a minimum 30 minutes fire resisting material.
- Access through a window and external ladder.

Walls, fences and gates

Building Regulations approval is required:

- If the walls, fences and gates are higher than 2m.
- If the walls, fences and gates adjoining a highway are higher than 1m.

All electrical work

Part P (Electrical Safety) of the Building Regulations now requires all electrical work to be carried out by certified people except very limited work.

Work that can be carried out by non-certified operatives:

- Replacement of light fittings, sockets, switches.
- Replacement of damaged cable for a single circuit.
- Work not in the bathroom and kitchen comprising;
    - Additional lighting, fittings and switches to existing circuit.
    - Additional sockets and fused spurs to existing ring or radial main.
    - Additional earth bonding.

These works are conditional upon:

- The use of suitable cable and fittings for the particular application.
- Circuit protective measures are unaffected and suitable for protecting the new circuit.
- All works comply with all other appropriate regulations.

Work that must be carried out by certified operatives:

- All new modifications to electrical wiring within bathrooms and shower rooms.
- Installation or modification to underfloor heating.

- Installation or modification to ceiling heating.
- Power or lighting to garden.
- Specialist installations.

DIY work

Building Regulations will apply equally to DIY work and work undertaken by a contractor. The Local Authority will need to be notified of DIY changes before the work is commenced. The work will be inspected and tested.

Certificates

You will need to keep the appropriate certificates from the Local Authority to prove that any work was approved. You will need to produce them when you come to sell the house.

Party Walls

If the property is a terraced or semi detached house then a wall (or walls if a mid terrace) will be shared with a neighbour. This shared wall is known as the party wall.

You must obtain your neighbours consent before any of the following building work is started:
- Extensions
- Structural alterations
- Some internal refurbishment
- Damp proofing works

In some cases, if excavations or constructing foundations for a new construction are within 3m or 6m of the neighbouring property, then written consent will also be required.

Your neighbour cannot in normal circumstances withhold consent, as long as the provisions of the Party Wall etc Act are followed.

The Party Wall etc. Act 1996

The Party Wall etc. Act 1996 produced a procedure for homeowners in England and Wales. It applies to all building work involving a party wall or party fence wall. The Act was designed to minimise disputes by ensuring property owners use a surveyor to determine the time and way in which the work is carried out.

An 'agreed surveyor' can be used to act for both owners should problems arise.

The Act covers the following and written agreement is required:
- Bearing of beam – cutting into wall for eg. a loft conversion or supporting upper floor after removal of a loadbearing internal wall.
- Damp proof course – inserting new all the way through the wall.

- Underpinning the party wall.
- Demolishing and rebuilding the party wall.
- Raising the whole party wall including cutting off any objects, if necessary preventing this from happening.
- Protecting adjoining walls by cutting a flashing into an adjoining building.
- Building a new wall on the line of the junction between two properties.
- Excavating foundations:
- Within 3m of an adjoining structure and lower than its foundation.
- Within 6m of an adjoining structure and below a line drawn down 45 degrees from the bottom of its foundation.

The Act does not cover the following and written agreement is not required:
- Minor works not affecting the neighbour's part of the party wall.
- Fixing plugs.
- Fixing skirting or other woodwork.
- Screwing in wall units.
- Screwing in shelving.
- Replastering walls.
- Adding or replacing electrical wiring or socket outlet.

Notice of party wall work
Written notice must be given to neighbours:
- **At least two months** before starting any party wall works.
- **One month** for building a wall between properties or excavation works.

If tenants or leaseholders live next door, the landlord must also be informed. Written notice must also be given to owners living above or below the property.

Endeavour to talk to neighbours before issuing notices as this can prevent any future problems.

Neighbours should give written approval within 14 days of receipt of the notice.

Disputes
If there is a dispute:
- Both parties appoint their own surveyor or
- Both parties appoint 'agreed surveyor'.

The surveyor will draw up the 'Award', a document which details work to be carried out, when and how it is to be done, and a record of the condition of the adjoining property before the work is started.

The Award will determine who will pay for the work if this is in dispute, although this is generally the property owner who started the work.

Party wall guidance
A useful guide, 'Party Wall Guidance' can be obtained free of charge from the Royal Institution of Chartered Surveyors. It provides information on party wall law and where you can go for advice. Visit: www.rics.org/partywalls.

Building Materials
The selection of buildings materials will be dependent upon the existing property, especially the external fabric. Another factor is how close it is to other buildings and how they are constructed. These factors affect the materials and design, particularly the front elevation/elevation facing the main road.

Building materials do have a bearing both when obtaining Planning, and Building Regulations approval. It is again recommended that you discuss selection before going ahead.

Where possible, and especially on the elevation facing the main road, the materials chosen for the external fabric such as bricks, roof tiles, windows, doors, should match or be sympathetic with the existing property.

Grants

There are a number of grants available to householders, some of which are listed below. They are obtained from Local Authorities and the householder is therefore recommended to contact them to discuss whether the work they envisage qualifies for a grant, what proportion of the cost may be given by the Authority, and the rules governing the award of a grant.

The law sets out a framework of all the various work that is eligible for a grant, however each authority may have their particular guidelines to determine what work has funding priority.

Renovation grants

This grant is discretionary and will be available for either large-scale works to make a house fit for habitation, or to put a house into reasonable repair.

These grants may be available if the house is in serious disrepair, deemed unfit to live in, and the owner cannot afford to pay for these repairs.

The types of work, which would be considered for a grant, are:
- Installing a fixed bath or shower, wash basin, sink, including

hot and cold water supply, and an inside toilet, where none previously existed in the building.
- Extensive dampness.
- Any work which has been instructed by the Local Authority, under a statutory notice or order:
  - If the property is in a serious state of disrepair.
  - If the property does not meet with their standards under law, eg no inside toilet.
  - If the property is in a Housing Action Area.
  - If the house is occupied by more than one family and a fire escape may be required.

Grant assistance is not available for routine repair and maintenance work, eg. repainting front door, renewing tap washer.

Authorities can award grants for work costing up to £20,000 in total. The grant will be set at 50% of the cost up to the £20,000 maximum.

Empty homes grants

These may be available from an authority and they are given to enable an empty property to be brought back into a habitable condition.

The grant available will vary with each authority, but will typically range from, £1000 or 50% of the cost of eligible works, up to a maximum of £5000 per habitable room.

Authorities may differ on their rules regarding the interpretation of 'empty', eg. a property has been empty for at least six months, a property has been unoccupied and no Council Tax has been paid for three months or more.

Disabled facilities grants

These are available for the adaptation of a property to meet the recommended disabled occupants health needs, eg. enlarging a separate toilet to enable wheelchair access and the fitting of grab rails.

Lead pipe replacement

Small grants may be separately available towards the replacement of lead supply pipes.

Insulation grants

These may be available to cover the cost of works to improve the thermal insulation of a property.

1.5 MAJOR PROPERTY PROBLEMS

When looking at a property it is important to consider the factors that may have contributed to problems as well as the problems themselves. In some circumstances, treating the symptoms not the disease can lead to problems reoccurring.

The causes of major property problems can be classified as follows:
- Original construction.
- Maintenance of building – poor maintenance of building once construction has been completed.
- Maintenance around building.
- Movement.
- Weather conditions.
- Finance.

Original Construction

Throughout the years there have been times when either labour and/or materials shortages, or the urgency to put up buildings while demand was strong, has lead to sub-standard construction and the use of sub-standard materials.

World wars and natural disasters also contribute, from time to time, in altering the standards of labour and materials.

For example:
Poor quality or undersized softwood used in the original construction can lead to the timber deteriorating. Initial poor preparation and decoration may further contribute to timber decay. This results in the need to repair or replace much earlier than might be expected.

Maintenance of the Building

Lack of maintenance can lead to major maintenance problems.

If repairs are not carried out when the problem first arises, other areas of the property can be affected thus exacerbating the problem.

For example:
A blocked gutter, if not cleared quickly, can cause the gutter joints and gutter itself to break. Water overflowing can cause dampness to penetrate the building. Staining to brickwork, whilst not a major problem, can become unsightly. Continued damp penetration will lead to wood rot in any timber in contact with the wall.

For example:
A lack of redecoration to external joinery, particularly where paint has fallen off or joints have shrunk, can cause problems with rot to the woodwork.

Maintenance around the Building

Problems can occur from the following:

Trees, shrubs:
- Root action can cause ground shrinkage, pressure in foundations and damage drains.
- Removal of a large tree can alter the ground conditions, causing below ground water problems and subsequently movement to the building.
- Trees and shrubs close to the building can cause damp to penetrate through the external fabric.
- Falling leaves block gutters and gullies. A build up against the external wall of the building can cause damp to penetrate through the external fabric.

- Structural damage - a large tree falling onto the building can cause structural damage. Large branches breaking off can also cause damage to the roof tiling etc.

Creepers: Climbing plants such as ivy
- Mortar failure between bricks in external walls.
- Damage to the face of brickwork.
- Damage to vertical boarding, fascias, rainwater gutters, roof tiling/slating including battens and felt, ie. anywhere that the creeper can grow between or into.
- Block outlets such as flues, extract and gas ventilators.

Ground level above dpc:
- Soil is allowed to bank up above the damp proof course (dpc), leading to damp penetration of solid walls.
- A footpath is constructed along the external wall at, or above, the height of the damp proof course.

Movement
Movement of the structure of a building can be caused by the building moving or the ground moving, either of which can create major structural problems and can be caused by:
- Inadequate foundations.
- Proximity of large trees.
- Adverse weather conditions.
- Changes to local ground conditions, eg by removal of large tree, changes to paving and/or hardstandings.
- Traffic - particularly applicable to older houses built along main roads and due to the increase in traffic in recent years, especially heavy goods lorries.

Weather Conditions
Adverse weather conditions such as heavy rain or periods of drought, can affect the structure of the ground and consequently movement damage can follow.

High winds can weaken parts of the structure such as roof tiling/slating, chimneys.

Finance
It may have occurred that, at the time a repair was necessary, funds were not available. A repair may then have been carried out using an inferior or inappropriate material and/or cheaper less skilled labour. This may have been deemed a temporary measure at the time, however, if the repair is not corrected at a later date then increased problems may arise.

For example:
The use of hard mortar or render to replace original lime mortar in old properties can lead to cracking to brickwork or damp retention behind the render.

PART TWO

2:1 REPAIRS

	Tiles/slates in One Location (m²)			
	1 £	2 £	5 £	6 £
AREAS OF TILES/SLATES MISSING OR BROKEN ON ROOF				
SOLUTION				
Replace missing/broken tiles/slates				
Plain clay tile	**280**	**360**	**385**	**465**
Concrete interlocking tile	**240**	**280**	**390**	**430**
Natural slate	**330**	**460**	**630**	**755**

	Tiles/slates in One Location (number)			
	1 £	2 £	5 £	6 £
INDIVIDUAL OR SEVERAL TILES/ SLATES MISSING OR BROKEN ON ROOF				
SOLUTION				
Replace missing/broken tiles/slates				
Plain clay tile	**225**	**240**	**255**	**265**
Concrete interlocking tile	**225**	**240**	**255**	**265**
Natural slate	**230**	**250**	**270**	**280**
INDIVIDUAL OR SEVERAL TILES/ SLATES LOOSE ON ROOF				
SOLUTION				
Resecure tiles/slates	**220**	**230**	**240**	**245**

	Area (m²)		
	10 £	15 £	25 £
FELT TO FLAT ROOF IS LEAKING			
Inspection recommends replacement			
SOLUTION			
Replace three layer felt roof	**515**	**680**	**990**
FELT TO FLAT ROOF IS LEAKING AND BOARDING IS DAMAGED			
Inspection recommends replacement			
SOLUTION			
Replace three layer felt roof and boarding	**685**	**1030**	**1700**
FELT TO FLAT ROOF IS LEAKING, BOARDING AND INSULATION IS DAMAGED			
Inspection recommends replacement			
SOLUTION			
Replace three layer felt roof, boarding and insulation	**1430**	**2140**	**3530**
ASPHALT TO FLAT ROOF IS LEAKING			
Inspection recommends replacement			
SOLUTION			
Hack up asphalt roofing and apply 19mm two coat work on felt and underlay.	**515**	**795**	**1350**
FELT TO FLAT ROOF IS LEAKING			
Inspection recommends replacement			
SOLUTION			
Prepare existing mastic asphalt and overlay with HP felt	**455**	**600**	**880**
Apply one coat bituminous paint	**250**	**290**	**365**
Apply two coats bituminous paint	**450**	**590**	**865**

	Repairs (number)		
	1 £	2 £	5 £

SMALL PATCHES IN TOP LAYER OF FELT ROOF ARE DAMAGED OR SPLIT

SOLUTION
Cut out defective layer, rebonding to adjacent layers and covering with single layer felt

	1 £	2 £	5 £
Small patches not exceeding 0.5m^2	195	220	280
0.5 - 2m^2	210	245	350
2 - 5m^2	250	325	555

SMALL DEPRESSIONS HAVE APPEARED IN ROOF DECK

SOLUTION

	1 £	2 £	5 £
Repair felt and boarding	225	270	420

AREA OF FELT ROOF IS DEVOID OF CHIPPINGS

SOLUTION
Clear stone chippings, dress surface with compound and recover with chippings

	1 £	2 £	5 £
Small patches not exceeding 0.5m^2	195	220	280
0.5 - 2m^2	200	220	295
2 - 5m^2	220	270	415

BLISTERS OR CRACKS IN ASPHALT

SOLUTION

	1 £	2 £	5 £
Cut out detached blister and make good, 0.5m^2 area	195	215	270
Cut out crack and make good, per m run	200	225	300

	Length of Flashing (m)			
	1	2	5	6
	£	£	£	£

ROOF LEAKING AT JUNCTION OF WALL AND ROOF

Inspection recommends replacement of lead flashing

SOLUTION

	1	2	5	6
Replace flashing up to 225mm girth	330	390	450	510
Replace stepped flashing up to 240mm girth	440	525	610	695
Parapet box gutter 650mm girth including boxed end, cover flashing, dress into rainwater head	1310	1650	1990	2300
Valley gutter 600mm wide	1680	2070	2460	2850

DAMP PATCH INTERNALLY AT TOP OF CHIMNEY BREAST

SOLUTION

Replace chimney flashing

	Length (mm)	
	700	1200
	£	£
Replace back gutter to chimney stack, 500mm girth	320	360

ROOF FLASHING IS CRACKED OR LOOSE

SOLUTION

Repair flashing.

	Length of Crack (m)			
	4	5	6	7
	£	£	£	£
Repair crack in sheeting, clean out and fill with solder	185	205	225	250
Refix existing lead flashings with new wedges and repoint with mortar	240	275	310	345

	Repairs (number)			
	1	2	3	5
	£	£	£	£
Repair crack not exceeding 150mm long and fill with solder	100	110	120	140
Repair crack not exceeding 150 to 300mm long and fill with solder	110	120	130	150

	RANGE House Type		
	Terraced £		Detached £

EAVES OR VERGE BOARDING IS LOOSE

SOLUTION

Resecure eaves fascia, including decoration

	Terraced		Detached
ONE ELEVATION	180	to	330
WHOLE HOUSE	310	to	1040

Resecure eaves soffit, including decoration

ONE ELEVATION	190	to	350
WHOLE HOUSE	330	to	1100

Resecure eaves fascia and soffit, including decoration

ONE ELEVATION	265	to	575
WHOLE HOUSE	480	to	1810

Resecure verge boarding, including decoration
One Side Elevation

ONE SIDE	220	to	275
BOTH SIDES	360	to	470

EXTERIOR
Replace Gutters, Rainwater Pipes or Fittings

	Length of Gutter/Pipe (m)		
	1	2	3
	£	£	£

GUTTERS ARE MISSING OR DAMAGED

SOLUTION
Replace gutters

	1	2	3
PVCu	110	140	170
Aluminium	120	165	210
Cast iron, including decoration	150	220	290

RAINWATER DOWN PIPES ARE MISSING OR DAMAGED

SOLUTION
Replace pipes

	1	2	3
PVCu	100	125	150
Aluminium	125	170	215
Cast iron, including decoration	160	240	320

	Fittings (number)		
	1	2	3
	£	£	£

RAINWATER FITTINGS ARE MISSING OR DAMAGED

SOLUTION
Replace head/hopper

	1	2	3
Cast aluminium, powder coated finish	100	150	200
Fabricated aluminium, powder coated finish	150	250	350
Cast iron, including decoration	91	130	170

Replace shoes

	1	2	3
PVCu	72	94	115
Aluminium	86	120	160
Cast iron	88	125	160

Replace balloon grating

	1	2	3
PVCu	56	63	70

Replace gutter brackets

	1	2	3
PVCu	56	63	70
Galvanised repair bracket	63	75	87

GUTTER JOINTS ARE LEAKING

SOLUTION
Repair joints

	Fittings (number)		
	1	2	3
	£	£	£
Apply mastic sealant to gutter joint	**61**	**72**	**83**

GUTTERS ARE OVERFLOWING

SOLUTION
Clean out or realign gutters and downpipes

		RANGE		
		House Type		
		Terraced		Detached
		£		£
Clean out gutters, outlets etc				
	ONE ELEVATION	**105**	to	**155**
	WHOLE HOUSE	**160**	to	**460**
Realign gutters				
PVCu				
	ONE ELEVATION	**195**	to	**405**
	WHOLE HOUSE	**340**	to	**1260**
Metal				
	ONE ELEVATION	**235**	to	**495**
	WHOLE HOUSE	**420**	to	**1560**
Realign down pipes				
PVCu				
	ONE ELEVATION	**190**	to	**210**
	TWO ELEVATIONS	**230**	to	**255**
Metal				
	ONE ELEVATION	**230**	to	**255**
	TWO ELEVATIONS	**410**	to	**460**

	Pots per Stack		RANGE	
		£		£

CHIMNEY STACK IN POOR CONDITION, LEANING
Inspection recommends rebuilding

SOLUTION
Rebuild stack 1m high, reset existing pots

	1	**1650**	to	**2040**
	2	**2040**	to	**2820**
	4	**2970**	to	**3600**

Rebuild stack 1m high, replace 450mm high pots

	1	**1720**	to	**2190**
	2	**2350**	to	**2970**
	4	**3440**	to	**4070**

Rebuild stack 1m high, replace 900mm high pots

	1	**1880**	to	**2350**
	2	**2660**	to	**3290**
	4	**4070**	to	**4700**

Rebuild stack 2m high, reset existing pots

	1	**2190**	to	**2820**
	2	**3290**	to	**4070**
	4	**3600**	to	**4540**

Rebuild stack 2m high, replace 450mm high pots

	1	**2350**	to	**2970**
	2	**3440**	to	**4380**
	4	**4070**	to	**5170**

Rebuild stack 2m high, replace 900mm high pots

	1	**2500**	to	**3130**
	2	**3760**	to	**4700**
	4	**4700**	to	**5790**

POINTING TO CHIMNEY STACK IN POOR CONDITION

SOLUTION
Repoint 1m high stack

	1	**565**	to	**610**
	2	**595**	to	**660**
	4	**610**	to	**705**

Repoint 2m high stack

	1	**640**	to	**750**
	2	**705**	to	**845**
	4	**750**	to	**940**

	Pots per Stack		
	1	2	4
	£	£	£

POINTING TO CHIMNEY STACK
FLASHINGS IN POOR CONDITION

SOLUTION
Repoint flashings at base of chimney stack

		1	2	4
Front or back flashing	ONE SIDE	**160**	**160**	**165**
Stepped flashing	ONE SIDE	**170**	**205**	**205**
All flashings around chimney	ALL SIDES	**225**	**260**	**270**

CHIMNEY POTS DAMAGED OR MISSING

SOLUTION
Replace pots and flaunching

	1	2	4
450mm high pot	**600**	**735**	**1000**
900mm high pot	**760**	**1050**	**1630**

	Single Items £

TV AERIAL IS LOOSE

SOLUTION

Refix aerial to chimney stack, including renewing fixings	**170**

EXTERIOR
Rebuild, Repoint, Dampproofing, Cleaning Brickwork

EXTERNAL WALLS REQUIRE REBUILDING

SOLUTION Rebuild external skin of cavity wall	ELEVATION	RANGE House Type		
		Terraced £		Detached £
Rebuild wall	FRONT OR REAR	**6190**	to	**22490**
Rebuild wall including new wall insulation batts	FRONT OR REAR	**6760**	to	**24270**
Rebuild wall including replacing polystyrene insulation	FRONT OR REAR	**6840**	to	**24550**
		Semi Detached £		Detached £
Rebuild wall	SIDE	**20350**	to	**21720**
Rebuild wall including new wall insulation batts	SIDE	**22230**	to	**23440**
Rebuild wall including replacing polystyrene insulation	SIDE	**22510**	to	**23700**

EXTERNAL BRICK WALLS REQUIRE REPOINTING

		RANGE House Type		
		Terraced £		Detached £
SOLUTION Repoint external wall				
	ONE ELEVATION	**680**	to	**1900**
	WHOLE HOUSE	**1360**	to	**6600**

DAMP IS PENETRATING THROUGH EXTERNAL WALL

There is no existing damp course or the damp course has failed

SOLUTION
Install hessian based damp proof course

	ONE ELEVATION	**285**	to	**910**
	WHOLE HOUSE	**580**	to	**2880**

Inject silicone damp proofing

	ONE ELEVATION	**165**	to	**445**
	WHOLE HOUSE	**260**	to	**1410**

		RANGE		
		House Type		
	ELEVATION	Terraced £		Detached £

EXTERNAL BRICK WALLS ARE DIRTY/STAINED

SOLUTION
Spray with water and brush lightly

	Terraced £		Detached £
ONE ELEVATION	**735**	to	**2070**
WHOLE HOUSE	**1470**	to	**8020**

Sandblast

ONE ELEVATION	**935**	to	**2700**
WHOLE HOUSE	**1870**	to	**10480**

BRICK FACES ARE DAMAGED OR CRACKED

	Area of Patch (m²)	RANGE Quality of Bricks		
		£		£

SOLUTION
Replace defective bricks at low level
(no scaffolding required)

Area of Patch (m²)	£		£
1	**185**	to	**275**
2	**275**	to	**450**
3	**405**	to	**680**
5	**675**	to	**1130**

Replace defective bricks at high level
(scaffolding required)

Area of Patch (m²)	£		£
1	**205**	to	**295**
2	**295**	to	**470**
3	**440**	to	**715**
5	**710**	to	**1170**

BRICKWORK HAS CRACK

SOLUTION
Cut out brickwork and replace with new brickwork at low level
(no scaffolding required)

Length of Crack (m)	£		£
1	**115**	to	**165**
2	**180**	to	**280**
3	**250**	to	**390**
5	**385**	to	**565**

Cut out brickwork and replace with new brickwork at high level
(scaffolding required)

Length of Crack (m)	£		£
1	**135**	to	**200**
2	**205**	to	**330**
3	**290**	to	**425**
5	**425**	to	**605**

Crack in Brickwork

Crack in Pointing

		RANGE		
		Quality of Bricks		
		£		£

INDIVIDUAL BRICKS ARE DAMAGED OR CRACKED

SOLUTION
Replace defective bricks at low level

	Bricks (number)			
	1	56	to	65
	2	65	to	70
	5	85	to	100
	10	120	to	150

Replace defective bricks at high level

	1	74	to	82
	2	82	to	87
	5	105	to	120
	10	140	to	170

HOLES IN BRICKWORK AFTER PIPES HAVE BEEN REMOVED

SOLUTION
Fill holes

	Holes (number)			
	1	2	3	5
	£	£	£	£
Half brick thick walls	75	85	95	115
One brick thick walls	81	95	110	135

POINTING TO BRICK WALLS IN POOR CONDITION

SOLUTION
Rake out joints and repoint

	RANGE		
	House Type		
	Terraced		Detached
	£		£
	£		£
ONE ELEVATION	680	to	3050
WHOLE HOUSE	1360	to	11880

POINTING TO SMALL AREAS OF
BRICK WALLS IN POOR CONDITION

SOLUTION
Repoint

	Area of Patch (m²)			
	1	2	3	5
	£	£	£	£
Pointing at low level				
Rake out joints and repoint by machine	105	150	190	285
Rake out joints and repoint by hand	115	160	205	325
Pointing at high level				
Rake out joints and repoint by machine	135	175	215	315
Rake out joints and repoint by hand	140	190	240	350

BRICKWORK IS STAINED

SOLUTION
Clean brickwork

	Area (m²)			
	1	2	5	10
	£	£	£	£
Cleaning at low level				
Sandblasting	85	120	225	400
Spraying with water	74	97	170	290
Cleaning at high level				
Sandblasting	105	145	290	530
Spraying with water	96	120	210	370

CRACK HAS APPEARED ALONG
POINTING IN BRICKWORK

SOLUTION
Repoint crack in joint

	Length of Crack (m)			
	1	2	3	5
	£	£	£	£
Pointing at low level				
Cut out crack and repoint to match existing	75	83	92	125
Pointing at high level				
Cut out crack and repoint to match existing	100	110	120	150

	Length of Pointing (m)			
	1	2	3	5
	£	£	£	£

POINTING HAS BECOME LOOSE ALONG FLASHING

SOLUTION
Repoint mortar along flashing
Pointing at low level

	1	2	3	5
Rake out joint and point in flashing	77	87	98	135

Pointing at high level

	1	2	3	5
Rake out joint and point in flashing	105	115	125	160

POINTING HAS BECOME LOOSE AROUND DOOR OR WINDOW FRAMES

SOLUTION
Repoint around frames
Pointing at low level

	1	2	3	5
Rake out joint and repoint in mortar or mastic	78	92	105	145

Pointing at high level

	1	2	3	5
Rake out joint and repoint in mortar or mastic	105	120	135	175

CRACKS AROUND LINTELS, INSUFFICIENT BEARING OR LINTEL HAS FAILED

	RANGE Size Variation		
	£		£

SOLUTION
Replace lintel at low level

	£		£
Replace concrete lintel	280	to	325
Replace steel lintel	300	to	410

Replace lintel at high level

	£		£
Replace concrete lintel	335	to	380
Replace steel lintel	360	to	465

EXTERIOR
Repointing and Cleaning Stonework, Repairs and Decorating to Rendering

	ELEVATION	RANGE House Type		
		Terraced £		Detached £
EXTERNAL STONE WALLS REQUIRE REPOINTING				
SOLUTION				
Repoint stone walls	ONE ELEVATION	935	to	3860
	WHOLE HOUSE	1870	to	15040
EXTERNAL STONE WALLS REQUIRE CLEANING				
SOLUTION				
Spray with water and brush lightly	ONE ELEVATION	820	to	2970
	WHOLE HOUSE	1640	to	11540
Sandblast	ONE ELEVATION	1020	to	3950
	WHOLE HOUSE	2040	to	15400
EXTERNAL RENDERING IS IN POOR CONDITION				
SOLUTION				
Rerender with two coats cement and sand render	ONE ELEVATION	1219	to	3590
	WHOLE HOUSE	2420	to	13980
EXTERNAL RENDERING DECORATION IS IN POOR CONDITION				
SOLUTION				
Prepare and apply one coat exterior cement paint	ONE ELEVATION	540	to	1450
	WHOLE HOUSE	1080	to	5580
EXTERNAL RENDERING DECORATION IS BADLY STAINED				
SOLUTION				
Prepare and apply one coat fungicidal treatment	ONE ELEVATION	510	to	1360
	WHOLE HOUSE	1020	to	5220
EXTERNAL PEBBLE DASH IS IN POOR CONDITION				
SOLUTION				
Replace pebbledash	ONE ELEVATION	1330	to	3950
	WHOLE HOUSE	2660	to	15400

	Small Patch n.e. 0.5m² (number) £	Area (m²)		
		1 £	2 £	5 £

RENDERING IS DAMAGED

SOLUTION
Repair rendering at low level
Two coats cement and sand render, decorated

| | 130 | 170 | 230 | 410 |

Repair rendering at high level
Two coats cement and sand render, decorated

| | 155 | 195 | 260 | 470 |

PEBBLE DASH IS DAMAGED

SOLUTION
Repair pebbledash at low level
Pebble dash finish

| | 130 | 155 | 210 | 370 |

Repair pebbledash at high level
Pebble dash finish

| | 160 | 185 | 240 | 430 |

	Area (m²)			
	1 £	2 £	5 £	10 £

BRICKWORK IS STAINED

SOLUTION
Cleaning at low level

| Sandblasting | 85 | 120 | 225 | 400 |
| Spraying with water | 74 | 97 | 170 | 290 |

Cleaning at high level

| Sandblasting | 105 | 145 | 290 | 530 |
| Spraying with water | 96 | 120 | 210 | 370 |

	Individual Board (number) £	Area (m²)		
		2 £	3 £	5 £

VERTICAL SHIPLAP CLADDING IS DAMAGED

SOLUTION
Replace cladding at low level

Replace softwood boarding	95	255	350	540
Replace pvc cladding	82	200	270	410

Replace cladding at high level

Replace softwood boarding	125	280	375	565
Replace pvc cladding	135	230	300	440

	Area (m²)			
	2 £	3 £	5 £	6 £

VERTICAL TILING IS MISSING OR DAMAGED

SOLUTION
Replace tiles or slates at low level

Replace vertical tiles	245	335	515	605
Replace vertical slates	375	570	960	1160

Replace tiles or slates at high level

Replace vertical tiles	280	370	555	640
Replace vertical slates	410	605	995	1190

	Tiles in One Location (number)		
	1 £	5 £	10 £

Replace tiles or slates at low level

Replace vertical tiles	98	140	190
Replace vertical slates	100	160	220

Replace tiles or slates at high level

Replace vertical tiles	125	170	220
Replace vertical slates	130	185	255

	RANGE Quality of Material	
	£	£

EXTERNAL DOOR IS DAMAGED

SOLUTION
Replace doors and frames as necessary

Replace external door
Remove door, hang new door including refixing ironmongery
and decoration to both sides

| | 330 | to | 515 |

Remove door, hang new door including new ironmongery
and decoration to both sides

| | 475 | to | 775 |

Replace doors and frames
Replace timber door and frame with PVCu
door and frame

| | 760 | to | 920 |

EXTERNAL DOOR IRONMONGERY IS NOT FUNCTIONING

SOLUTION
Replace external door ironmongery

	£		£
Renew rim lock and SAA lever furniture	72	to	96
Renew steel butts, one and half pairs	90	to	125
Renew mortice deadlock	87	to	145
Renew cylinder mortice latch	150	to	240
Renew letter plate	93	to	105

GLASS TO DOOR IS BROKEN OR CRACKED

SOLUTION
Hack out broken glass and putty and reglaze single door

	£		£
One pane size 150 x 150mm in half glazed panel door	55	to	56
All panes size 150 x 150mm in half glazed panel door	77	to	105
Half glazed panel door	81	to	100
Fully glazed panel door	130	to	170

	Single Items £
PUTTY IS MISSING OR DAMAGED	
SOLUTION Replace putty	
One pane size 150 x 150mm in half glazed panel door	**51**
All panes size 150 x 150mm in half glazed panel door	**78**
Half glazed panel door	**54**
Fully glazed panel door	**56**
GLAZING BEADS ARE MISSING OR DAMAGED	
SOLUTION Replace glazing beads including decoration	
One pane size 150 x 150mm in half glazed panel door	**60**
All panes size 150 x 150mm in half glazed panel door	**190**
Half glazed panel door	**69**
Fully glazed panel door	**83**

	Single Items £

DOORS AND FRAMES DAMAGED OR NOT CLOSING, THRESHOLDS UNSATISFACTORY

SOLUTION
Repair doors and frames

Ease door without removal	**56**
Take down door, ease, adjust and rehang	**67**
Take down door, shave 12mm from bottom edge and rehang	**67**
Remove door, shave sides and top and bottom edges to fit opening, rehang	**91**

Ease and adjust doors and frames

Ease and adjust door and frame of any size, adjust door stops, refix architraveand frame, overhaul ironmongery and leave in good working order	**87**

Repair/replace door frames and thresholds
Take off door and rehang, remove and refix ironmongery as necessary, make good decorations and leave in good working order

Repair single door and frame of any size	**130**
Replace softwood door frame	**260**
Replace hardwood threshold	**205**

Replace water bar

Galvanised steel bar bedded in mastic, to single door opening	**100**

Repoint one side with polysulphide sealant

Single door frame	**67**
Threshold	**54**

Insert external threshold seal with weather board strip

Single door opening	**87**
Single door opening to doors with water bar	**125**

	RANGE Approx Window Size (mm)	
	600 x 900 £	1200 x 1200 £

WINDOW IS DAMAGED OR ROTTEN

SOLUTION
Replace window at low level

Take out and install new double glazed window

PVCu casement window	220	to	565
PVCu sash window	850	to	1580

Take out and install new double glazed window including decorating externally

Timber casement window	445	to	630
Timber sash window	665	to	1060
Metal casement window	510	to	675

Replace window at high level

Take out and install new double glazed window

PVCu casement window	275	to	620
PVCu sash window	905	to	1630

Take out and install new double glazed window including decorating externally

Timber casement window	500	to	690
Timber sash window	720	to	1120
Metal casement window	565	to	730

	Approx Window Size (mm)	Single Items £
WINDOW IS DAMAGED OR ROTTEN		
SOLUTION		
Replace window at low level		
Take out and install new double glazed window		
PVCu casement window	1800 x 1800	**1270**
PVCu sash window	1800 x 1800	**3550**
Take out and install new double glazed window including decorating externally		
Timber casement window	1800 x 1800	**1420**
Timber sash window	1800 x 1800	**2380**
Metal casement window	1800 x 1800	**1520**
Replace window at high level		
Take out and install new double glazed window		
PVCu casement window	1500 x 1200	**790**
PVCu sash window	1500 x 1200	**2060**
Take out and install new double glazed window including decorating externally		
Timber casement window	1500 x 1200	**875**
Timber sash window	1500 x 1200	**1410**
Metal casement window	1500 x 1200	**930**
OPENING WINDOW IS STICKING		
SOLUTION		
Ease opening casement or sash without removal		**56**
Renew sash cord to single sash		**85**
Renew both sets of sash cords to single window		**92**
SECONDARY GLAZING UNIT DOES NOT OPERATE		
SOLUTION		
Remove and refit unit, of any size		**60**

	Single Items £
OPENING WINDOWS AND IRONMONGERY STICKING, PUTTY AND BEADS ROTTEN OR MISSING	
SOLUTION	
Ease and adjust casement or sash window, overhaul ironmongery, renew beads with putty and sprigs, adjust stops and beads	**90**
WINDOW IN POOR CONDITION	
SOLUTION	
Piece in damaged area of frame, sill or casement with new timber, renew broken glass as necessary, overhaul or provide new ironmongery	**160**
WINDOW SILL IS ROTTEN	
SOLUTION	
Cut out sill complete and replace, including decoration	
600mm long	**150**
1800mm long	**270**
POINTING AROUND WINDOW FRAME IS MISSING OR LOOSE	
SOLUTION	
Repoint frame, up to window size 1800 x 1800mm	**74**
Repoint window sills 600 - 1800mm long	**56**
SEALS AROUND SASH WINDOWS ARE MISSING OR DAMAGED	
SOLUTION	
Install seal to window size 650 x 1050	**170**
Install seal to window size 900 x 1200	**205**
IRONMONGERY TO WINDOW IS MISSING OR INOPERABLE	
SOLUTION	
Renew casement stay and fastener	**70**
Renew sash fastener	**66**
Renew cast iron sash weight	**96**

	RANGE Approx Pane Size (mm)		
	300 x 600 £		900 x 900 £

WINDOW PANE IS BROKEN

SOLUTION
Remove glass and putty, prepare and reglaze   **87**   to   **180**

PUTTY AROUND PANE IS MISSING OR LOOSE

SOLUTION
Replace putty   **56**   to   **61**

PROBLEM
Glazing beads around pane are missing or damaged

SOLUTION
Replace glazing beads including decoration   **78**   to   **105**

	Canopy Area 750mm x		
	1200mm £	1950mm £	3000mm £
ENTRANCE CANOPY IS DAMAGED			
SOLUTION			
Replace canopy			
Softwood framed canopy with roof tiles on plywood	**485**	**785**	**1250**
GRP canopy with tile effect roof	**315**	**405**	**625**

	RANGE House Type		
	Terraced £		Detached £

MAJOR CRACKS AND/OR BOWING IN EXTERNAL WALL

SOLUTION

	Terraced		Detached
Structural report recommended	**750**	to	**1000**

Report states that foundations of property should be underpinned

UNDERPIN

Underpin including removing and later reinstating soil

		Terraced		Detached
	ONE WALL	**2100**	to	**6300**
	WHOLE HOUSE	**4200**	to	**20000**

Underpin including breaking up and later reinstating concrete paving

		Terraced		Detached
	ONE WALL	**2300**	to	**6800**
	WHOLE HOUSE	**4500**	to	**21500**

MINOR CRACKS IN EXTERNAL WALLS

		RANGE Quality of Bricks		
		£		£

SOLUTION
Replace damaged bricks to external wall

Replace, at low level

	Area of brickwork m²			
Area of brickwork	1	**185**	to	**275**
	2	**275**	to	**450**
	3	**405**	to	**680**
	5	**675**	to	**1130**

	Length of crack m			
Length of crack	1	**115**	to	**165**
	2	**180**	to	**280**
	3	**250**	to	**390**
	5	**385**	to	**565**

	Individual bricks number			
Individual bricks	1	**56**	to	**64**
	2	**64**	to	**69**
	5	**85**	to	**99**
	10	**120**	to	**150**

	RANGE Quality of Bricks	
	£	£

MINOR CRACKS IN EXTERNAL WALLS

SOLUTION

Replace damaged bricks to external wall

Replace, at high level

	Area of brickwork m²		
Area of brickwork	1	**205** to	**295**
	2	**295** to	**470**
	3	**440** to	**715**
	5	**710** to	**1170**

	Length of crack m		
Length of crack	1	**135** to	**200**
	2	**205** to	**330**
	3	**290** to	**425**
	5	**425** to	**605**

	Individual bricks number		
Individual bricks	1	**74** to	**82**
	2	**82** to	**87**
	5	**105** to	**120**
	10	**140** to	**170**

DAMP PENETRATING WALL AT LOW LEVEL
**Ground level is above the existing damp proof
course (dpc)**

SOLUTION
Excavate as necessary to ensure that finished
ground level is a minimum 150mm below the
existing damp proof level, remove soil and
consolidate, to a minimum width of one metre

		Terraced £		Detached £
		RANGE House Type		
Excavate soil only				
	ONE WALL	150	to	325
	WHOLE HOUSE	200	to	1080
Excavate soil and lay new gravel path				
	ONE WALL	170	to	385
	WHOLE HOUSE	240	to	1270
Excavate soil and lay precast concrete paving slabs				
	ONE WALL	320	to	770
	WHOLE HOUSE	540	to	2440
Excavate soil and lay 100mm thick concrete path, with formwork to edge, to falls, tamped finish				
	ONE WALL	390	to	990
	WHOLE HOUSE	680	to	3130

	1 £	2 £	3 £	5 £
	Length (m)			
Excavate soil only	84	105	130	170
Excavate soil and lay new gravel path	89	115	145	195
Excavate soil and lay precast concrete paving slabs	125	190	255	380
Excavate soil and lay 100mm thick concrete path, with formwork to edge, to falls, tamped finish	145	225	310	475

DAMP PENETRATING WALL AT LOW LEVEL
No damp proof course in wall

SOLUTION
Cut out two courses of brickwork and insert hessian damp proof course, pointing in mortar and making good brickwork or inject silicone damp proofing

	RANGE		
		House Type	
	Terraced		Detached
	£		£
Install hessian based bitumen damp proof course			
ONE WALL	**295**	to	**890**
WHOLE HOUSE	**590**	to	**2820**
Inject silicone damp proofing			
ONE WALL	**160**	to	**420**
WHOLE HOUSE	**320**	to	**1470**

DAMP PENETRATING SOLID
EXTERNAL WALL AND PLASTER

SOLUTION
Apply one coat exterior waterproof compound to brickwork, concrete, rendered surfaces

	Area (m²)			
	1	2	3	5
	£	£	£	£
One coat exterior waterproof compound	**72**	**83**	**94**	**115**

DAMP PENETRATING PLASTER/WALL
OF CAVITY WALL

SOLUTION
Clean out blocked cavities from outside, include cutting out facing bricks, clearing mortar droppings and renewing bricks to match existing

	Number of Locations			
	1	2	3	5
	£	£	£	£
Clean out cavities by removing three bricks	**110**	**160**	**210**	**310**

**DAMP PENETRATION THROUGH
WALLS AT VARIOUS LOCATIONS,
AROUND WINDOWS AND DOORS,
AT CEILING HEIGHT**

SOLUTION
Insert damp proof course

	Length (m)			
	1 £	2 £	3 £	5 £
Work to cavity walls at low level				
Cut out one course of bricks in any quality facing bricks, in short lengths (approximately 675mm) and insert polypropylene refurbishment cavity tray, renew facings to match existing	130	200	265	400
Cut out one stepped course bricks, any quality facing bricks, and insert combined cavity dpc preformed polypropylene and lead cavity tray, renew bricks to match existing	205	270	430	715
Take off copings, prepare wall, insert damp proof course and relay coping	110	155	200	290
Work to cavity walls at high level				
Cut out one course of bricks in any quality facing bricks, in short lengths (approximately 675mm) and insert polypropylene refurbishment cavity tray, renew facings to match existing	150	220	290	445
Cut out one stepped course bricks, any quality facing bricks, and insert combined cavity dpc preformed polypropylene and lead cavity tray, renew bricks to match existing	230	295	455	760
Take off copings, prepare wall, insert damp proof course and relay coping	130	175	220	315

INTERNAL WALLS ARE DAMP

SOLUTION
Hack off existing plaster, rake out joints in
brickwork/blockwork for key, apply three coat
asphalt tanking, cement and sand render and refix
or install new skirting to match existing, decorate
wall

	RANGE House Type		
	Terraced £		Detached £
Asphalt tanking to 1.2m high (decorate full height)			
ONE WALL	**1170**	to	**3500**
WHOLE HOUSE	**2340**	to	**11080**
Asphalt tanking to full height of ground floor wall			
ONE WALL	**2440**	to	**7310**
WHOLE HOUSE	**4880**	to	**23140**

	Floors to Room Room Size		
	3 x 3m £	4 x 4m £	8 x 4m £
Asphalt tanking to 1.2m high (decorate full height)	**2570**	**3740**	**5150**
Asphalt tanking to full height of ground floor wall	**6560**	**8990**	**14520**

GROUND FLOORS ARE DAMP

SOLUTION
Remove flooring, screed and skirting from
room, lay 500 gauge bitumen coated
polyethylene membrane and priming, or two
coat asphalt tanking, reinstate screed and refix
skirting

		RANGE House Type		
		Terraced £		Detached £
Bitumen coated polyethylene membrane	WHOLE HOUSE	**1650**	to	**9840**
Mastic asphalt tanking	WHOLE HOUSE	**1980**	to	**11800**

		RANGE		
		Bitumen £		Mastic Asphalt £
	Room Size			
Lay tanking and reinstate screed only				
	3 x 3 m	**710**	to	**850**
	4 x 4m	**1260**	to	**1510**
	8 x 4m	**2520**	to	**3020**
Lay tanking, reinstate screed and lay new flooring				
	3 x 3 m	**1310**	to	**1770**
	4 x 4m	**2330**	to	**3140**
	8 x 4m	**4660**	to	**6290**

WALLS TO KITCHEN OR BATHROOM
ARE DAMP

SOLUTION
Install extract fan in external wall, including
forming hole through cavity, or glass to window

	RANGE Quality of Fan		
	£		£
Install extract fan	**235**	to	**380**

INSULATION IN ROOF AREA IS DAMAGED OR MISSING

SOLUTION
Clear out insulation and vacuum roof space and lay 250mm thick glass fibre insulation

RANGE			
House Type			
Terraced			Detached
£			£
525		to	**3130**

Length (m)			
1	2	3	5
£	£	£	£
75	**100**	**125**	**175**

INSUFFICIENT THICKNESS OF INSULATION
250mm thick is recommended

SOLUTION
Lay 150mm thick glass fibre insulation over existing insulation

RANGE			
House Type			
Terraced			Detached
£			£
345		to	**1760**

Length (m)			
1	2	3	5
£	£	£	£
64	**78**	**92**	**120**

DIFFICULTY WITH ACCESS ACROSS ROOF SPACE

SOLUTION
Install 1m wide timber flooring as walkways

Length of Walkway (m)	Plywood £	RANGE	Softwood £
1	**73**	to	**145**
2	**97**	to	**210**
3	**120**	to	**290**
5	**165**	to	**400**

	Terraced £	RANGE House Type	Detached £

IMPROVE INSULATION LEVEL TO EXTERNAL WALLS

SOLUTION
Inject cavity wall with foam or mineral fibre system

	Terraced £		Detached £
	220	to	**2060**

IMPROVE INSULATION LEVEL TO PANELLED EXTERNAL WALLS

SOLUTION
Hack off render, replace or install new insulation panel with rigid insulation board and metal lathing and rerender to match existing

ONE WALL	**3490**	to	**10880**
WHOLE HOUSE	**6980**	to	**42680**

As above but including one coat exterior stone paint to render

ONE WALL	**3690**	to	**11520**
WHOLE HOUSE	**7380**	to	**45200**

	Walls 2.75m High Length (m)			
	3 £	4 £	5 £	8 £

IMPROVE INSULATION LEVEL TO WALLS

SOLUTION

	3	4	5	8
Take down plasterboard to internal skin, install insulation, fix new plasterboard, skim coat and decorate	**370**	**510**	**650**	**1020**
Construct plasterboard timber stud partition with insulation, plasterboard, skim coat, skirting and decoration to one side	**1040**	**1430**	**1820**	**2850**

WATER TANK INSULATION MISSING OR DAMAGED

SOLUTION
Replace insulating jacket

	RANGE Per Jacket		
	£		£
Replace insulating jacket around cold water tank	**200**	to	**250**
Replace insulating jacket around hot water cylinder	**90**	to	**110**

INSULATION TO PIPEWORK IS DAMAGED OR MISSING

SOLUTION
Replace insulation to pipework

	Length of Pipework(m)			
	1 £	2 £	5 £	10 £
Replace pipe insulation in roof space or cupboards	**60**	**70**	**95**	**140**
Replace pipe insulation to pipes under floors, pipes running in direction of floor boarding	**65**	**80**	**120**	**190**
Replace pipe insulation to pipes under floors, pipes running in opposite direction of floor boarding	**95**	**140**	**270**	**480**

**INSUFFICIENT VENTILATION
IN ROOF SPACE**

SOLUTION
Improve ventilation

		RANGE House Type		
		Terraced £		Detached £
Remove tile or slate from roof slope and install tile vents		**200**	to	**1200**
Form hole in boarding at eaves and install ventilator at 1m centres				
	ONE ELEVATION	**95**	to	**160**
	TWO ELEVATIONS	**140**	to	**240**
Form hole in boarding at eaves and install continuous plastic ventilator				
	ONE ELEVATION	**120**	to	**240**
	TWO ELEVATIONS	**190**	to	**400**
Remove ridge tiles and install ridge vent at 2m centres, with adaptor, make good all work disturbed		**210**	to	**860**

	Vents (number)			
	2 £	4 £	6 £	8 £
Remove tile or slate from roof slope and install tile vents	**335**	**480**	**650**	**750**
Remove ridge tiles and install ridge vent at 2m centres, with adaptor, make good all work disturbed	**545**	**900**	**1100**	**1450**

SECTION OF ROOF TIMBER IS DECAYED OR DAMAGED

SOLUTION
Cut out existing decayed, split etc. timber and splice in softwood treated timber

	Length of Timber (m)		
	1	2	3
	£	£	£
Rafters or purlins	**130**	**205**	**280**
Ridges	**135**	**220**	**305**

WHOLE OF ROOF TIMBERS ARE DECAYED OR DAMAGED

SOLUTION
Replace existing decayed, split etc. timber and splice in softwood treated timber

	Length of Timber (m)		
	4	5	6
	£	£	£
Rafters or purlins	**310**	**390**	**470**
Ridges	**345**	**430**	**515**

VENTILATE FLOORS TO PREVENT FUTURE DAMAGE TO TIMBER

SOLUTION
Ventilation is recommended to prevent further decay

Install louvred ventilator in internal wall and air brick in external wall
NOTE: air bricks should be located at 1.8m intervals along external walls

		RANGE Quality of Bricks		
	Number of bricks	£		£
Solid or cavity wall	1	**120**	to	**155**
	2	**175**	to	**250**
	3	**235**	to	**345**
	5	**300**	to	**475**

FLOOR JOISTS ARE ROTTEN OR SPLIT

SOLUTION
Replace 50 x 150mm floor joist

	Length of Timber (m)			
	1	2	3	5
	£	£	£	£
Take up floor boards, renew joist, refix boards	90	130	170	250
Take up flooring, renew joist, lay new softwood boarded flooring	155	255	295	505
Take up flooring, renew joist, lay new chipboard flooring	105	165	220	335
Replace 50 x 225mm floor joist				
Take up floor boards, renew joist, refix boards	100	150	200	300
Take up flooring, renew joist, lay new softwood boarded flooring	165	275	390	555
Take up flooring, renew joist, lay new chipboard flooring	115	185	250	385

TIMBER FLOOR IS TOO SPRINGY

SOLUTION
Install 50 x 30mm softwood herringbone strutting between existing joists

	Lengths of Strutting (m)			
	1	2	3	5
	£	£	£	£
Take up floor boards, install strutting, refix boards	70	91	110	150
Take up flooring, renew joist, lay new softwood boarded flooring	100	145	170	240
Take up flooring, renew joist, lay new chipboard flooring	94	140	180	270
Install 100 x 50mm softwood solid strutting between existing joists				
Take up floor boards, renew joist, refix boards	72	93	115	160
Take up flooring, renew joist, lay new softwood boarded flooring	99	135	160	225
Take up flooring, renew joist, lay new chipboard flooring	120	195	265	350

TIMBER FLOOR AND JOISTS ARE DECAYED OR DAMAGED

SOLUTION
Take up flooring to expose joists, treatment as necessary, refix or replace flooring, treat flooring and/or joists

	Number of Floors	Terraced £	RANGE House Type	Detached £
Treat timber floor/joists				
Apply water repellant preservative				
To softwood flooring	Both floors	180	to	840
	One floor	120	to	420
To softwood flooring and joists	Both floors	780	to	5560
	One floor	390	to	2780
Apply woodworm treatment				
To timber flooring	Both floors	205	to	1020
	One floor	135	to	510
To timber flooring and joists	Both floors	870	to	6200
	One floor	435	to	3100
Replace timber flooring				
Softwood butt jointed boards	Both floors	2070	to	14690
	One floor	1035	to	7345
Softwood tongued and grooved boards	Both floors	2240	to	15950
	One floor	1120	to	7975
Chipboard flooring, butt jointed	Both floors	795	to	5660
	One floor	400	to	2830
Chipboard flooring, tongued and grooved joints	Both floors	965	to	6860
	One floor	480	to	3430

TIMBER FLOOR AND JOISTS ARE DECAYED

SOLUTION
Take up flooring to expose joists, treatment as necessary

Treat timber floor/joists

	Floors to Room Room Size		
	3 x 3m	4 x 4m	8 x 4m
	£	£	£
Apply water repellant preservative			
To softwood flooring	95	120	175
To softwood flooring and joists	270	365	735
Apply woodworm treatment			
To timber flooring	100	130	200
To timber flooring and joists	290	410	820

	Area of Flooring (m^2)			
	1	2	3	5
	£	£	£	£
Apply water repellant preservative				
To softwood flooring	65	69	72	79
To softwood flooring and joists	85	110	130	175
Apply woodworm treatment				
To timber flooring	66	70	74	83
To timber flooring and joists	85	115	140	190

TIMBER FLOOR IS BADLY DAMAGED

SOLUTION
Take up and replace flooring

Replace timber flooring

	Floors to Room Room Size		
	3 x 3m £	4 x 4m £	8 x 4m £
Softwood butt jointed boards	545	970	1940
Softwood tongued and grooved boards	595	1060	2110
Chipboard flooring, butt jointed	270	375	750
Chipboard flooring, tongued and grooved joints	320	455	910

	Area of Flooring (m²)			
	1 £	2 £	3 £	5 £
Softwood butt jointed boards	145	205	280	425
Softwood tongued and grooved boards	155	220	300	465
Chipboard flooring, butt jointed	96	120	150	205
Chipboard flooring, tongued and grooved joints	105	130	165	230
Hardboard, fixed with nails	76	90	105	130
Plywood fixed with nails	85	110	130	180

TIMBER JOISTS ARE DECAYED OR DAMAGED

SOLUTION
Take up flooring to expose joists, replace joists, refix or replace flooring

	Area of Flooring (m²)			
	1 £	2 £	3 £	5 £
Take up floor boards, renew joist, refix boards				
Softwood butt jointed boards	100	135	175	250
Softwood tongued and grooved boards	105	140	180	260
Take up flooring, renew joist, lay new flooring				
Softwood butt jointed boards	155	255	345	475
Softwood tongued and grooved boards	165	270	370	515
Chipboard flooring, butt jointed	115	165	220	320
Chipboard flooring, tongued and grooved joints	120	175	230	345

FLOOR IS SCORED AND DIRTY

SOLUTION
Sand or cover floor to whole room

		Terraced £	RANGE House Type	Detached £
Clean and sand boarded floor				
	GROUND FLOOR	485	to	2900
	FIRST FLOOR	395	to	2800
	WHOLE HOUSE	880	to	5700
Lay hardboard on existing timber floor				
	GROUND FLOOR	320	to	1870
	FIRST FLOOR	240	to	1810
	WHOLE HOUSE	560	to	3680
Lay plywood on existing timber floor				
	GROUND FLOOR	490	to	2930
	FIRST FLOOR	400	to	2840
	WHOLE HOUSE	890	to	5770

	Floors to Room Room Size		
	3 x 3m £	4 x 4m £	8 x 4m £
Sand or cover floor to whole room			
Clean and sand boarded floor	260	370	740
Lay hardboard to surface of existing timber floor, fix with nails	185	290	580
Lay plywood to surface of existing timber floor, fix with nails	260	375	750

**FLOOR BOARDS ARE LOOSE
AND UNEVEN**

SOLUTION
Lift and refix softwood floorboards

		RANGE		
		House Type		
	Terraced			Detached
	£			£
GROUND FLOOR	310	to		2150
FIRST FLOOR	240	to		2080
WHOLE HOUSE	550	to		4230

	Floors to Room		
	Room Size		
	3 x 3m	4 x 4m	8 x 4m
	£	£	£
Softwood boarded flooring throughout room	205	325	550

	Area of Flooring (m²)			
	1	2	3	5
	£	£	£	£
Softwood boarded flooring, in small areas	67	84	100	135

	Height of Flue (m)			
	5 £	6 £	11 £	12 £
FLUE LINING MISSING				
SOLUTION				
Repair cracks				
Line flue with concrete flue linings				
First floor flue	315	340	—	—
Ground floor flue	—	—	390	405

	Number of Chimneys	
	1 £	2 £
DAMP IS PENETRATING THROUGH WALLS OF SEALED CHIMNEY STACK		
SOLUTION		
Cut opening in bricked up chimney breast, provide and fix plaster louvre ventilator size 150 x 225mm	83	115
CHIMNEY FLUE IS BLOCKED		
SOLUTION		
Sweep chimney	54	78

	Single Items £

SEVERE CRACKING OVER FIREPLACE OPENING

SOLUTION

Replace lintol over opening, make good plaster and emulsion paint	**530**

MANTLE IS DAMAGED

SOLUTION

Replace pine mantle	**325**
Replace micro marble mantle	**800**

HEARTH IS DAMAGED

SOLUTION

Replace hearth with Decostone	**325**
Replace hearth with conglomerate marble	**380**

FIREPLACE IS DAMAGED

SOLUTION

Replace with conglomerate marble back panel and hearth, pine mantle	**610**
Replace with green marble or black granite back panel and hearth, stone micro marble mantle	**2040**

FIREBACK IS DAMAGED

SOLUTION

Replace fireback for solid fuel fire	**200**
Replace fireback for gas fire	**230**

	RANGE	
	Quality of Materials	
	£	£

INTERNAL DOOR IS DAMAGED OR MISSING

SOLUTION

Replace flush door, reuse existing ironmongery, decorate	**200**	to	**325**
Replace flush door, fix new ironmongery, decorate	**240**	to	**420**
Replace six panel door, reuse existing ironmongery, decorate	**365**	to	**600**
Replace six panel door, fix new ironmongery, decorate	**405**	to	**690**

Single
Items
£

DOOR IS STICKING AND DOES NOT OPEN/CLOSE EASILY

SOLUTION
Ease sticking doors

Ease door without removal	**56**
Take down door, ease, adjust and rehang	**67**
Take down door, shave from bottom edge and rehang	**67**
Remove door, shave sides and top and bottom edges to fit opening, rehang	**91**
Ease and adjust door and frame of any size, adjust door stops, refix architrave and frame, overhaul ironmongery and leave in good working order	**80**

DOOR IS DAMAGED

SOLUTION
Repair door

Take down panelled door of any size, remove ironmongery and cover both sides with hardboard, refix ironmongery, adjust stops, rehang and decorate	**130**

DOOR FRAME IS DAMAGED OR LOOSE

SOLUTION

Take off door, remove ironmongery as necessary, replace door frame, decorate, refix door and ironmongery and leave in good working order	**230**
Take off door, remove ironmongery as necessary, replug and refix frame or lining, decorate, refix door and ironmongery and leave in good working order	**145**

	RANGE Type of Glass		
	£		£

GLAZING TO DOOR IS BROKEN

SOLUTION
Hack out broken glass and putty and reglaze single door

One pane size 150 x 150mm in half glazed panel door	**55**	to	**56**
All panes size 150 x 150mm in half glazed panel door	**77**	to	**105**
Half glazed panel door	**81**	to	**100**
Fully glazed panel door	**130**	to	**170**

	Single Items £

PUTTY OR GLAZING BEADS ARE MISSING
OR LOOSE

SOLUTION
Replace putty

One pane size 150 x 150mm in half glazed panel door	**51**
All panes size 150 x 150mm in half glazed panel door	**78**
Half glazed panel door	**54**
Fully glazed panel door	**56**

Replace glazing beads including decoration	
One pane size 150 x 150mm in half glazed panel door	**60**
All panes size 150 x 150mm in half glazed panel door	**190**
Half glazed panel door	**69**
Fully glazed panel door	**83**

	Single Items £

STAIRCASE TREADS, RISER, BALUSTERS ARE BADLY DAMAGED

SOLUTION
Replace

Straight flight softwood staircase	**1060**
Softwood handrail to stair flight	**175**
Softwood turned newel post	**125**
Hardwood turned newel post	**150**

HANDRAIL IS LOOSE

SOLUTION
Refix

Take off and refix handrail between newel posts	**61**

STAIRCASE TREADS, RISER, BALUSTERS ARE DAMAGED

SOLUTION
Repair

	Number of Units			
	1 £	2 £	3 £	5 £
Replace tread or riser to staircase	**80**	**110**	**140**	**200**
Replace plain baluster	**75**	**100**	**125**	**175**
Replace ornate baluster	**80**	**110**	**140**	**200**
Replug and screw handrail brackets	**58**	**65**	**73**	**88**

	Length of Worktop (m)			
	1 £	2 £	3 £	5 £

WORKTOP IS BADLY SCORED/CHIPPED

SOLUTION
Replace worktop

	1	2	3	5
500mm wide	115	180	245	375
600mm wide	125	200	275	425

LAMINATE EDGING IS LOOSE OR MISSING

SOLUTION

	1	2	3	5
Replace plastic laminate edging 25mm wide	58	66	74	90

	Number of Units			
	1 £	2 £	3 £	5 £

DOORS OR DRAWERS ARE DAMAGED

SOLUTION
Replace

	1	2	3	5
Replace damaged door using existing ironmongery	255	385	595	955
Replace damaged drawer to floor unit to match existing	185	320	455	725

DOORS OR DRAWERS ARE BADLY FITTING

SOLUTION
Repair

	1	2	3	5
Take off, ease adjust and rehang door	62	73	84	105
Repair drawer, refix front and runners	67	85	100	135
Refix drawer, ease and adjust including runners	56	62	68	80

EXTERNAL DRAINAGE
Rainwater - Above Ground

	Length (m)		
	1	2	3
GUTTERS ARE MISSING OR DAMAGED	£	£	£

SOLUTION
Replace gutters

PVCu	110	140	170
Aluminium	120	165	210
Cast iron, including decoration	150	220	290

RAINWATER DOWN PIPES ARE MISSING OR DAMAGED

SOLUTION
Replace pipes

PVCu	100	125	150
Aluminium	125	170	215
Cast iron, including decoration	160	240	320

RAINWATER FITTINGS ARE MISSING OR DAMAGED

SOLUTION
Replace head/hopper

Cast aluminium, powder coated finish	100	150	200
Fabricated aluminium, powder coated finish	150	250	350
Cast iron, including decoration	90	130	170

Replace shoes

PVCu	72	94	115
Aluminium	86	120	160
Cast iron	88	125	160

Replace balloon grating

PVCu	56	63	70

Replace gutter brackets

PVCu	56	63	70
Galvanised repair bracket	63	75	87

	Fittings (number)		
	1	2	3
GUTTER JOINTS ARE LEAKING	£	£	£

SOLUTION
Apply mastic sealant to gutter joint

	1	2	3
	61	**72**	**83**

	RANGE		
	House Type		
	Terraced		Detached
GUTTERS ARE OVERFLOWING	£		£

SOLUTION
Clean out gutters, outlets etc

	Terraced		Detached
ONE ELEVATION	**105**	to	**155**
WHOLE HOUSE	**160**	to	**460**

Realign gutters
PVCu

ONE ELEVATION	**195**	to	**405**
WHOLE HOUSE	**340**	to	**1260**

Metal

ONE ELEVATION	**235**	to	**495**
WHOLE HOUSE	**420**	to	**1560**

Realign down pipes
PVCu

ONE ELEVATION	**190**	to	**210**
TWO ELEVATIONS	**230**	to	**255**

Metal

ONE ELEVATION	**230**	to	**255**
TWO ELEVATIONS	**410**	to	**460**

	Single Items £

**NO SOAKAWAY TO RAINWATER DOWNPIPE
OR EXISTING SOAKAWAY OF INSUFFICIENT SIZE**

SOLUTION
Enlarge or form new soakaway
Excavate pit approx 1000 x 1000 x 1200mm, fill with selected hardcore and
top with concrete bed on polythene sheeting and sand blinding **260**

	Length (m)		
	1	2	5
	£	£	£

SOIL DOWN PIPES ARE MISSING OR DAMAGED

SOLUTION

	1	2	5
Replace pipes with PVCu pipework	**80**	**110**	**200**

	Single Items £

TRAPS TO SOIL PIPES ARE DAMAGED/BROKEN

SOLUTION
Replace

	Single Items £
32mm bottle trap and joints	**66**
40mm bottle trap and joints	**85**

BLOCKAGES OR OBSTRUCTIONS IN SANITARY FITTINGS

SOLUTION
Unblock

Clear obstruction or blockage from WC pan, bath, shower, basin or sink, clean wastes and traps including removal and reassembling as necessary	**100**

	Single Items £

SEPTIC TANK IS LEAKING

SOLUTION
Replace

Excavate by hand, pit around existing tank, remove and install new septic tank, fixing lockable manhole cover and frame and connect to pipework
3750 litre capacity 2000mm diameter standard grade, 1000 mm depth to invert ... **2440**
3750 litre capacity 2000mm diameter heavy duty grade, 1500 mm depth to invert ... **3340**

DRAINS MAY BE BLOCKED

SOLUTION
Inspect drains

CCTV survey of drains including video and report, any reasonable run of domestic pipework ... **145**

DRAINS ARE BLOCKED

SOLUTION
Clear obstructions in drain runs by water jetting, any reasonable run of domestic pipework ... **120**

Rod drain from manhole, clean out and flush through, including replacing and resealing manhole cover
Drain run not exceeding 30m ... **95**
Drain run over 30m ... **110**

	Length of Pipe (m)			
	1 £	2 £	3 £	5 £

DRAIN PIPES ARE BROKEN/CRACKED

SOLUTION
Replace broken length of vitrified or plastic pipe

100mm pipe

	1	2	3	5
Excavate through soft surface, average excavation depth 500mm deep, replace pipe, make good ground	120	185	250	330
Excavate through concrete or paving or tarmac surface, average excavation depth 500mm deep,replace pipe, make good surface to match existing	170	290	345	580
Excavate through soft surface, average excavation depth 1000mm deep, replace pipe, make good ground	145	240	335	525
Excavate through concrete or paving or tarmac surface, average excavation depth 1000mm deep, replace pipe, make good surface to match existing	195	340	490	780
Line damaged drain runs by inversion moulding, with grp lining	58	66	74	90

150mm pipe

	1	2	3	5
Excavate through soft surface, average excavation depth 500mm deep, replace pipe, make good ground	145	245	345	470
Excavate through concrete or paving or tarmac surface, average excavation depth 500mm deep, replace pipe, make good surface to match existing	195	345	425	720
Excavate through soft surface, average excavation depth 1000mm deep, replace pipe, make good ground	175	295	355	600
Excavate through concrete or paving or tarmac surface, average excavation depth 1000mm deep, replace pipe, make good surface to match existing	225	335	505	850
Line damaged drain runs by inversion moulding with grp lining	73	97	120	165

	Single Items £

MANHOLE COVER AND FRAME ARE LOOSE

SOLUTION
Take off manhole cover not exceeding 600 x 600mm,
lift up frame and rebed on top of manhole in cement
mortar (1:3), reseal cover — **90**

MANHOLE COVER AND FRAME ARE DAMAGED

SOLUTION
Renew damaged manhole cover and frame

Light duty cover and frame, clear opening 600 x 600mm	**205**
Medium duty cover and frame, clear opening 600 x 450mm	**205**
Medium duty cover and frame, clear opening 600 x 600mm	**225**

BENCHING AT BOTTOM OF MANHOLE IS LOOSE/MISSING

SOLUTION
Break out defective benching to bottom of manhole and renew
in cement mortar trowelled smooth

460 x 690mm internally	**135**
690 x 1140mm internally	**160**

MANHOLE HAS COLLAPSED OR IS IN PROCESS OF COLLAPSING

SOLUTION
Take up existing cover and frame, demolish manhole and rebuild
concrete base, engineering brick sides in cement mortar,
concrete benching 100mm diameter vitrified clay channel bends,
not exceeding 2nr, 600 x 450mm manhole cover and frame

600 x 450 x 750mm deep internally	**660**
600 x 450 x 1000mm deep internally	**825**

	Single Items £
GULLY IS BLOCKED	
SOLUTION Clean out blockage	**62**
GULLY GRID IS MISSING OR DAMAGED	
SOLUTION Replace cast iron gully grid	**60**
GULLY KERB IS DAMAGED	
SOLUTION Replace broken precast concrete gully kerb	**100**
GULLY IS DAMAGED	
SOLUTION Break out existing gully and install new back inlet gully with grating, connect to existing 100mm drain, surround with concrete	**350**
FRESH AIR INLET IS BROKEN OR MISSING	
SOLUTION Renew broken or missing aluminium fresh air inlet including mud flap	**125**

	Length of Drive/Footpath (m)			
DRIVEWAY IS BROKEN UP	5 £	10 £	15 £	20 £

SOLUTION
Replace driveway

Replace single width driveway

	5	10	15	20
75mm two coat rolled bitumen macadam	625	1250	1880	2500
Precast concrete slabs, 600 x 600	750	1500	2250	3000
Precast concrete coloured blocks, 200 x 100	1310	2620	3930	5240
Clay brick paviours 75mm thick (PC £35/100)	1370	2740	4110	5480
Clay brick paviours 25mm thick (PC £25/100)	1270	2540	3810	5080
Crazy paving broken precast concrete paving slabs	1310	2620	3930	5240
100mm thick insitu concrete with formwork to edges, to falls, tamped finish and trowelled edge	915	1830	2750	3660

Replace double width driveway

	5	10	15	20
75mm two coat rolled bitumen macadam	1250	2500	3750	5000
Precast concrete slabs, 600 x 600	1500	3000	4500	6000
Precast concrete coloured blocks, 200 x 100	2610	5220	7830	10440
Clay brick paviours 75mm thick (PC £35/100)	2740	5480	8220	10960
Clay brick paviours 25mm thick (PC £25/100)	2530	5060	7590	10120
Crazy paving broken precast concrete paving slabs	2630	5260	7890	10520
100mm thick insitu concrete with formwork to edges, to falls, tamped finish and trowelled edge	1830	3660	5490	7320

FOOTPATH IS BROKEN UP

SOLUTION
Replace footpath

Replace footpath 1.2m wide

	5	10	15	20
75mm two coat rolled bitumen macadam	300	500	750	1000
Precast concrete slabs, 600 x 600 x 50mm	375	600	900	1200
Precast concrete coloured blocks, 200 x 100	525	1050	1570	2100
Clay brick paviours 75mm thick (PC £35/100)	550	1100	1640	2200
Clay brick paviours 25mm thick (PC £25/100)	505	1010	1520	2020
Crazy paving broken precast concrete paving slabs	525	1050	1580	2100
75mm thick insitu concrete with formwork to edges, to falls, tamped finish and trowelled edge	350	700	1050	1400

	Length of Drive/Footpath (m)			
SURFACE OF DRIVEWAY IS BROKEN UP	5 £	10 £	15 £	20 £

SOLUTION
Replace surfacing to driveway

Replace surfacing to single width driveway

75mm two coat rolled bitumen macadam	460	920	1380	1840
Precast concrete slabs, 600 x 600 x 50mm	580	1160	1740	2320
Precast concrete coloured blocks, 200 x 100	1140	2280	3420	4560
Clay brick paviours 75mm thick (PC £35/100)	1200	2410	3620	4820
Clay brick paviours 25mm thick (PC £25/100)	1100	2200	3300	4400
Crazy paving broken precast concrete paving slabs	1150	2300	3450	4600
100mm thick insitu concrete with formwork to edges, to falls, tamped finish, trowelled edge	750	1500	2250	3000
Take up and relay precast concrete slabs on dabs	495	985	1480	1970

Replace surfacing to double width driveway

75mm two coat rolled bitumen macadam	915	1830	2750	3660
Precast concrete slabs, 600 x 600 x 50mm	1160	2320	3480	4640
Precast concrete coloured blocks, 200 x 100	2280	4560	6840	9120
Clay brick paviours 75mm thick (PC £35/100)	2410	4820	7230	9640
Clay brick paviours 25mm thick (PC £25/100)	2200	4400	6600	8800
Crazy paving broken precast concrete paving slabs	2290	4580	6870	9160
100mm thick insitu concrete with formwork to edges, to falls, tamped finish and trowelled edge	1500	3000	4500	6000

FOOTPATH IS BROKEN UP

SOLUTION
Replace surfacing to footpath

Replace surfacing to footpath 1.2m wide

75mm two coat rolled bitumen macadam	235	365	550	735
Precast concrete slabs, 600 x 600 x 50mm	295	465	695	925
Precast concrete coloured blocks, 200 x 100	455	910	1370	1820
Clay brick paviours 75mm thick (PC £35/100)	480	965	1450	1930
Clay brick paviours 25mm thick (PC £25/100)	440	880	1320	1760
Crazy paving broken precast concrete paving slabs	460	915	1375	1830
75mm thick insitu concrete with formwork to edges, to falls, tamped finish, trowelled edge	345	565	845	1130

DRIVEWAY OR FOOTPATH IS CRACKED

SOLUTION
Repair cracks

	Length of Crack (m)			
	1	2	3	5
	£	£	£	£
Fill crack in macadam or asphalt paving with hot bitumen	**150**	**160**	**170**	**185**
Rake out joint in brick paviors and repoint	**160**	**175**	**190**	**225**

DRIVEWAY OR FOOTPATH HAS POTHOLES

SOLUTION
Repair potholes

	Patches (number)			
	1	2	3	5
	£	£	£	£
Fill pothole in macadam or asphalt paving including preparing, making up levels and surfacing with mastic asphalt and limestone aggregate				
Small holes up to 0.1m^2	**82**	**98**	**115**	**145**
Large holes up to 1m^2	**130**	**200**	**270**	**415**

	Patches (number)			
	1	2	3	5
	£	£	£	£

DRIVEWAY OR FOOTPATH IS DAMAGED

SOLUTION
Repair damage to driveway or footpath

	1	2	3	5
Take up and renew precast concrete paving slabs				
Patches, individual slabs	85	105	125	160
Patches, three slabs	125	180	235	350
Patches, five slabs	140	215	290	440
Take up and renew reconstructed stone paving slabs				
Patches, individual slabs	87	105	125	170
Patches, three slabs	130	190	250	390
Patches, five slabs	200	345	475	665
Take up and renew coloured concrete block patches, individual blocks	99	130	165	230
Patches, five blocks	230	405	490	815
Patches not exceeding 0.2m²	90	115	135	185
Patches 0.2 to 0.5m²	125	180	235	370
Patches 0.5 to 1m²	180	295	420	570
Take up and renew brick paving				
Patches not exceeding 0.2m²	165	265	380	500
Patches 0.2 to 0.5m²	115	160	205	285
Patches 0.5 to 1m²	150	230	325	415

TREES OR SHRUBS ARE TOO CLOSE TO BUILDING AND ARE CAUSING DAMP OR CRACKING TO WALLS

SOLUTION
Remove trees or shrubs

	Single Items £
Cut down and remove small trees and shrubs	**375**
Cut down and remove large trees	**910**
Excavate around and remove tree stumps	
Small trees	**160**
Large trees	**240**

BRANCHES ARE OVERHANGING BUILDING, DRIVEWAY OR FOOTPATHS

SOLUTION
Cut back trees and shrubs

	Branches (number)			
	1 £	2 £	3 £	5 £
Pruning small branches not exceeding 1m long	**52**	**53**	**58**	**81**
Pruning large branches exceeding 1m long	**53**	**56**	**66**	**115**

BOUNDARY WALL IS FALLING DOWN

SOLUTION
Re-build freestanding brick wall

	Length of Wall (m)			
	1 £	2 £	3 £	5 £
Half brick thick wall				
1m high	160	270	380	550
1.5m high	220	385	505	840
2m high	270	445	665	1110
One brick thick wall				
1m high	260	425	635	1060
1.5m high	370	635	955	1590
2m high	425	850	1270	2120

RENDERING TO BOUNDARY WALL IS CRACKED OR LOOSE

SOLUTION
Repair rendering

	Length of Wall (m)			
	1 £	5 £	10 £	20 £
Hack off cracked and loose rendering and cart away, rake out joints and apply render				
1m high	120	350	705	1410
1.5m high	155	530	1060	2130
2m high	190	705	1410	2820

	Length of Fence (m)			
	1	5	10	20
	£	£	£	£

FENCING IS FALLING DOWN

SOLUTION
Replace fencing

Replace galvanised chain link fencing, with reinforced concrete posts

900mm high	145	485	970	1940
1200mm high	155	530	1060	2120

Replace galvanised chain link fencing to existing posts

900mm high	70	150	255	410
1200mm high	72	160	270	440

Replace chestnut pale fencing, softwood posts

1000mm high with 2 or 3 wires	140	445	890	1780

Replace close boarded fencing

Softwood posts	145	470	940	1880
Oak posts	155	525	1050	2100
Reinforced concrete posts	170	595	1190	2380

Replace interwoven panel fencing

Softwood posts	145	470	940	1880
Oak posts	160	555	1110	2220
Reinforced concrete posts	175	630	1260	2520

Replace gravel boards

Replace gravel boards with treated boards	62	115	165	260

	Panels or Posts (number)			
	1 £	2 £	3 £	5 £

FENCE PANELS ARE DAMAGED

SOLUTION
Replace interwoven or timber lap fencing

2m long panel and capping

	1	2	3	5
1m high	92	135	175	255
2m high	110	170	230	350

FENCE POSTS ARE BROKEN OR DAMAGED

SOLUTION
Replace intermediate post

2m long overall post

	1	2	3	5
Softwood	69	88	105	145
Oak	73	97	120	165
Concrete	83	115	150	215

GATES ARE MISSING, BROKEN OR DAMAGED

SOLUTION
Replace gates and posts

	Single Items £
Ledged and braced matchboard gate, including ironmongery	405
Framed, ledged and braced matchboard gate, including ironmongery	485
Single gate and posts, decorated, including stops and ironmongery	220
Double gates and posts, decorated, including ironmongery and stops, centre stop set in concrete	375

PART OF ROOF TIMBER IS DAMAGED
OR SPLIT

SOLUTION
Install softwood treated timber splints 1m long nailed to
both sides of existing damaged member

	Repairs (number)			
	1	2	4	6
	£	£	£	£
Rafters or purlins	81	115	175	235
Ridges	89	125	205	285

PART OF ROOF TIMBER IS DECAYED
OR SPLIT

SOLUTION
Cut out existing decayed, split etc. timber and
splice in softwood treated timber

	Length of Timber (m)		
	1	2	3
	£	£	£
Rafters or purlins	130	205	280
Ridges	135	220	305

COMPLETE ROOF TIMBER IS DECAYED
OR SPLIT

SOLUTION
Replace existing decayed, split etc. timber and
splice in softwood treated timber

		Length of Each Member (m)		
		4	5	6
		£	£	£
Rafters	single member	280	350	420
	two members	565	705	845
Purlins	single member	310	390	470
	two members	625	780	935

		Length of Each Member (m)		
		5	6	9
		£	£	£
Ridges		430	515	775

PART OF ROOF IS SAGGING

SOLUTION
Strengthen roof

Install additional softwood treated timber purlins

		Length of Each Member (m)		
		4	5	6
		£	£	£
Purlins	single member	155	180	205
	two members	250	295	340

Install additional softwood treated timber struts
or ties

		Length of Each Member (m)		
		2	3	4
		£	£	£
	single strut	110	130	150
	two struts	160	205	250

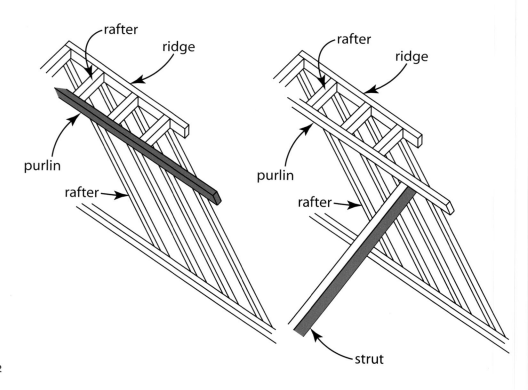

TILES/SLATES MISSING OR BROKEN ON ROOF

SOLUTION
Replace missing/broken tiles/slates

	Tiles/slates in One Location (m²)			
	1	2	5	6
	£	£	£	£
Plain clay tile	260	340	365	445
Concrete interlocking tile	220	260	370	410
Natural slate	310	440	610	735

	Tiles/slates in One Location (number)			
	1	2	5	6
	£	£	£	£

TILES/SLATES MISSING OR BROKEN ON ROOF

SOLUTION
Replace missing/broken tiles/slates

Plain clay tile	205	220	235	245
Concrete interlocking tile	205	220	235	245
Natural slate	210	230	250	260

TILES/SLATES LOOSE ON ROOF

SOLUTION
Resecure tiles/slates

	200	210	220	225

GARAGES AND OUTBUILDINGS
Roof Coverings

	Single Garage		Double Garage	
	Small £	Large £	Small £	Large £
FELT TO FLAT ROOF IS LEAKING Inspection recommends replacement				
SOLUTION Replace three layer felt roof	590	960	1130	1830
FELT TO FLAT ROOF IS LEAKING AND BOARDING IS DAMAGED Inspection recommends replacement				
SOLUTION Replace three layer felt roof and boarding	1240	2040	2420	3990
FELT TO FLAT ROOF IS LEAKING, BOARDING AND INSULATION IS DAMAGED Inspection recommends replacement				
SOLUTION Replace three layer felt roof, boarding and insulation	2540	4200	5020	8310
ASPHALT TO FLAT ROOF IS LEAKING Inspection recommends replacement				
SOLUTION Hack up asphalt roofing and apply 19mm two coat work on felt and underlay	990	1620	1920	3150
FELT TO FLAT ROOF IS LEAKING Inspection recommends replacement				
SOLUTION Prepare existing mastic asphalt and overlay with				
High performance felt	590	960	1130	1830
Apply one coat bituminous paint	280	440	505	800
Apply two coats bituminous paint	590	960	1130	1830

	Repairs (number)		
	1	2	5
	£	£	£

SMALL PATCHES IN TOP LAYER OF FELT ROOF ARE DAMAGED

SOLUTION
Cut out defective layer, rebond to adjacent layers and cover with single layer felt

Small patches not exceeding 0.5m²	195	220	280
0.5 - 2m²	210	245	350
2 - 5m²	250	325	555

SMALL DEPRESSIONS HAVE APPEARED IN ROOF DECK

SOLUTION
Repair felt and boarding

	225	270	420

AREAS OF FELT ROOF DEVOID OF CHIPPINGS

SOLUTION
Clear stone chippings, dress surface with compound and recover with chippings

Small patches not exceeding 0.5m²	195	220	280
0.5 - 2m²	200	220	295
2 - 5m²	220	270	415

BLISTERS OR CRACKS IN ASPHALT

SOLUTION

Cut out detached blister and make good, 0.5m² area	195	215	270
Cut out crack and make good, per m run	200	225	300

ROOF IS LEAKING AT JUNCTION
OF HOUSE AND GARAGE
Inspection recommends replacement of
lead flashing

SOLUTION

	Length (m)			
	3	5	6	10
	£	£	£	£
Replace flashing up to 225mm girth	**270**	**390**	**450**	**685**

ROOF IS LEAKING
Inspection recommends repair of lead flashing

SOLUTION

	Length (m)			
	1	2	3	5
	£	£	£	£
Repair crack in sheeting, clean out and fill with solder	**125**	**145**	**165**	**205**
Refix existing lead flashings with new wedges and repoint with mortar	**140**	**170**	**205**	**275**

	Repairs (number)			
	1	2	3	5
	£	£	£	£
Repair crack not exceeding 150mm long and fill with solder	**100**	**110**	**120**	**140**
Repair crack not exceeding 150 - 300mm long and fill with solder	**110**	**120**	**130**	**150**

EAVES OR VERGE BOARDING IS LOOSE

SOLUTION
Refix

	Single Garage		Double Garage	
	Small	Large	Small	Large
	£	£	£	£
Resecure eaves fascia, including decoration	**205**	**320**	**280**	**405**
Resecure eaves soffit, including decoration	**215**	**340**	**300**	**435**
Resecure eaves fascia and soffit, including decoration	**340**	**500**	**420**	**670**

	Single Garage		Double Garage	
	One Side	Both Sides	One Side	Both Sides
	£	£	£	£
Resecure verge boarding, including decoration	**130**	**170**	**170**	**245**

		RANGE (Quality of Bricks)		
		£		£

BRICK FACES ARE DAMAGED OR CRACKED

SOLUTION

Replace defective bricks

Area of Patch (m²)			
1	**205**	to	**295**
2	**295**	to	**470**
3	**440**	to	**715**
5	**710**	to	**1170**

BRICKWORK HAS CRACK

SOLUTION

Cut out brickwork and replace with new brickwork

Length of Crack (m)			
1	**115**	to	**165**
2	**180**	to	**280**
3	**250**	to	**390**
5	**385**	to	**565**

INDIVIDUAL BRICKS ARE DAMAGED OR CRACKED

SOLUTION

Replace defective bricks

Bricks (number)			
1	**56**	to	**65**
2	**65**	to	**70**
5	**85**	to	**100**
10	**120**	to	**150**

HOLES IN BRICKWORK AFTER PIPES HAVE BEEN REMOVED

SOLUTION

	Holes (number)			
	1	2	3	5
	£	£	£	£
Fill holes Half brick thick walls	**75**	**85**	**95**	**115**

POINTING TO BRICK WALLS
IN POOR CONDITION

SOLUTION
Repoint

		Single Garage		Double Garage	
		Small	Large	Small	Large
		£	£	£	£
Rake out joints and repoint					
	Front	**280**	**280**	**545**	**545**
	Rear	**425**	**425**	**770**	**770**
	Side	**855**	**1425**	**855**	**1425**
	All Walls	**2410**	**3550**	**3020**	**4160**

POINTING TO SMALL AREAS OF
BRICK WALLS IN POOR CONDITION

SOLUTION
Repoint

	Area of Patch (m²)			
	1	2	3	5
	£	£	£	£
Pointing				
Rake out joints and repoint by machine	**110**	**150**	**190**	**270**
Rake out joints and repoint by hand	**115**	**160**	**210**	**310**

	Small Patch n.e. 0.5m² (number) £	Area (m²)		
		1 £	2 £	5 £
RENDERING IS DAMAGED				
SOLUTION Repair render				
Hack out damaged render and rerender including decoration to match existing	130	170	230	410
PEBBLE DASH IS DAMAGED				
SOLUTION Repair pebble dash finish	130	155	210	370
BRICKWORK IS STAINED				
SOLUTION Sandblasting	85	120	225	400
Spraying with water	74	97	170	290

VERTICAL SHIPLAP CLADDING IS DAMAGED

SOLUTION
Replace damaged cladding

	Individual Board (number) £	Area (m²)		
		2 £	3 £	5 £
Replace softwood boarding	95	255	350	540
Replace pvc cladding	82	200	270	410
Replace softwood boarding	125	280	375	565
Replace pvc cladding	135	230	300	440

VERTICAL TILING IS MISSING OR DAMAGED

SOLUTION

	Area (m²)			
	2 £	3 £	5 £	6 £
Replace vertical tiles	245	335	515	605
Replace vertical slates	375	570	960	1160

	Tiles in One Location (number)		
	1 £	5 £	10 £
Replace vertical tiles	98	140	190
Replace vertical slates	100	160	220

CONCRETE FLOOR IS CRACKED

	Length of Crack (m)			
	1	2	3	5
	£	£	£	£
SOLUTION				
Clean out dust and debris and fill crack with mortar	55	61	66	77
Cut out crack to form groove and fill with mortar				
25 x 25mm groove	61	72	81	105
40 x 40mm groove	66	81	97	130

		RANGE	
	£		£

EXTERNAL DOOR IS DAMAGED

SOLUTION
Replace external door

Remove door, hang new door including refixing ironmongery and decoration to both sides	330	to	515
Remove door, hang new door including new ironmongery and decoration to both sides	475	to	775
Replace doors and frames			
Replace timber door and frame with PVCu door and frame	760	to	920

EXTERNAL DOOR IRONMONGERY IS NOT FUNCTIONING

SOLUTION
Replace external door ironmongery

Renew rim lock and SAA lever furniture	72	to	96
Renew steel butts, one and half pairs	90	to	125
Renew mortice deadlock	87	to	145
Renew cylinder mortice latch	150	to	240
Renew letter plate	93	to	105

GLASS TO DOOR IS BROKEN OR CRACKED

SOLUTION
Hack out broken glass and putty and reglaze single door

One pane size 150 x 150mm in half glazed panel door	55	to	56
All panes size 150 x 150mm in half glazed panel door	83	to	105
Half glazed panel door	81	to	99
Fully glazed panel door	130	to	170

GARAGE DOOR IS DAMAGED

Single Items
£

SOLUTION

Dismantle up and over door, supply and fit new aluminium door and decorate	1330
Take off doors and cart away, hang new framed, ledged and braced softwood doors, clad one side with v-jointed boarding and including furniture, new frame and decorations	1280

	Single Items £

PUTTY OR GLAZING BEADS ARE MISSING OR LOOSE

SOLUTION
Replace putty

One pane size 150 x 150mm in half glazed panel door	51
All panes size 150 x 150mm in half glazed panel door	78
Half glazed panel door	54
Fully glazed panel door	56

Replace glazing beads including decoration

One pane size 150 x 150mm in half glazed panel door	60
All panes size 150 x 150mm in half glazed panel door	190
Half glazed panel door	69
Fully glazed panel door	83

DOORS AND FRAMES DAMAGED OR NOT CLOSING, THRESHOLDS UNSATISFACTORY

SOLUTION
Repair doors and frames

Ease door without removal	56
Take down door, ease, adjust and rehang	67
Take down door, shave 12mm from bottom edge and rehang	67
Remove door, shave sides and top and bottom edges to fit opening, rehang	91

Ease and adjust doors and frames

Ease and adjust door and frame of any size, adjust door stops, refix architrave and frame, overhaul ironmongery and leave in good working order	87

Repair/replace door frames and thresholds
Take off door and rehang, remove and refix ironmongery as necessary, make good decorations and leave in good working order

Repair single door and frame of any size	130
Replace softwood door frame	260
Replace hardwood threshold	205

Replace water bar

Galvanised steel bar bedded in mastic, to single door opening	100

Repoint one side with polysulphide sealant

Single door frame	67
Threshold	54

Insert external threshold seal with weather board strip

Single door opening	87
Single door opening to doors with water bar	125

	RANGE		
	Approximate Window Size		
	600 x 900mm		1200 x 1200mm
	£		£

WINDOW IS DAMAGED OR ROTTEN

SOLUTION
Replace window

Take out and install new double glazed window			
PVCu casement window	220	to	565
PVCu sash window	850	to	1580
Take out and install new single glazed window including decorating externally			
Timber casement window	320	to	450
Timber sash window	590	to	925
Metal casement window	330	to	540
Take out and install new double glazed window including decorating externally			
Timber casement window	445	to	630
Timber sash window	665	to	1060
Metal casement window	510	to	675

	Single Items £
OPENING WINDOWS ARE STICKING	
SOLUTION	
Ease opening casement or sash without removal	**56**
Renew sash cord to single sash	**85**
Renew both sets of sash cords to single window	**92**
SECONDARY GLAZING UNIT DOES NOT OPERATE	
SOLUTION	
Remove and refit unit, of any size	**60**
OPENING WINDOWS AND IRONMONGERY STICKING, PUTTY AND BEADS ROTTEN OR MISSING	
SOLUTION	
Ease and adjust casement or sash window, overhaul ironmongery, renew beads with putty and sprigs, adjust stops and beads	**90**
WINDOW IN POOR CONDITION	
SOLUTION	
Piece in damaged area of frame, sill or casement with new timber, renew broken glass as necessary, overhaul or provide new ironmongery	**160**
WINDOW SILL IS ROTTEN	
SOLUTION	
Cut out sill complete and replace, including decoration	
600mm long	**150**
1800mm long	**270**
POINTING AROUND WINDOW FRAME IS MISSING OR LOOSE	
SOLUTION	
Repoint frame, up to window size 1800 x 1800mm	**74**
Repoint window sills, 600 - 1800mm long	**56**

IRONMONGERY TO WINDOW IS MISSING OR INOPERABLE

	Single Items £
SOLUTION	
Renew casement stay and fastener	**70**

WINDOW PANE IS BROKEN

	RANGE Approximate Pane Size		
	300 x 600mm £		900 x 900mm £
SOLUTION			
Remove glass and putty, prepare and reglaze	**76**	to	**135**

PUTTY AROUND PANE IS MISSING OR LOOSE

SOLUTION			
Replace putty	**56**	to	**61**

GLAZING BEADS AROUND PANE ARE MISSING OR DAMAGED

SOLUTION			
Replace glazing beads including decoration	**78**	to	**105**

2:2 SERVICES

ELECTRICITY

	Fittings (number)			
	1 £	2 £	3 £	5 £

CIRCUIT TO APPLIANCE IS FAULTY
Inspection recommends rewiring

SOLUTION

	1	2	3	5
Rewire circuit, from heater to fuse box, maximum cable length 12m	150	270	390	630
Rewire circuit, from heater to power connection, maximum cable length 3m	77	120	165	245
Renew thermostat	94	155	215	335

	Length of Cable/Conduit (m)			
	1 £	2 £	3 £	5 £

CIRCUIT TO POWER POINT/LIGHT POINT IS FAULTY
Inspection recommends rewiring

SOLUTION

	1	2	3	5
Renew wiring to power or lighting, in conduit	45	55	65	85

	Fittings (number)			
	1 £	2 £	3 £	5 £

FITTINGS ARE FAULTY
Inspection recommends rewiring

SOLUTION

	1	2	3	5
Refix power point including checking and reconnecting wiring	48	61	73	99
Replace damaged surface mounted socket outlet	65	95	125	185
Replace damaged flush mounted socket outlet cover plate only	62	89	115	170
Replace damaged flush mounted socket outlet including box	72	110	145	215

	Single Items £

FITTINGS ARE FAULTY
Inspection recommends replacing/overhauling

SOLUTION
Power

Faulty consumer control unit	
Overhaul and check consumer control unit	**46**
Renew consumer control unit	**255**
Renew MCB in existing consumer unit	**52**
Replace damaged fittings	
Renew cooker control panel, flush fitting	**82**

Lighting

Overhaul faulty lighting main switch including isolating and reconnecting supply, cleaning contacts and testing	**65**
Trace fault on wiring circuit	**62**

Replace faulty equipment

Renew time control switch and test	**120**
Renew immersion heater, isolate supply, drain tank, disconnect and connect heater and test top heater	**82**
Bottom heater	**98**
Instant water heaters	
Inspect and repair faulty heater	**60**
Supply and fit new instant hand wash unit	**260**

EXTERNAL WATER MAIN INSIDE PROPERTY BOUNDARY IS LEAKING

SOLUTION
Replace pipe

	Length of Pipework (m)			
	5	10	15	20
	£	£	£	£
Replace pipe, excavating and making good in the following surfaces				
Soft surface	340	560	780	1120
Concrete or paving slabs surface	440	880	1320	1760
Tarmac surface	480	960	1440	1920
Clay paviors surface	530	1060	1590	2120

	Length of Pipework (m)			
	1	2	3	5
	£	£	£	£
Replace short length of pipe, excavating and making good in the following surfaces				
Soft surface	105	160	215	345
Concrete or paving slabs surface	140	225	320	440
Tarmac surface	145	240	335	480
Clay paviors surface	155	260	365	530

WATER SUPPLY PIPEWORK INSIDE PROPERTY IS LEAKING
Inspection recommends total replacement

SOLUTION

	RANGE		
	£		£
Replace all hot and cold water pipework, storage cistern, expansion tank, hot water cylinder, immersion heater, connecting pipework to existing sanitary fittings	1940	to	2920
As above, but including new sanitary fittings	3850	to	8150

	Length of Pipework (m)			
	1	2	5	10
	£	£	£	£

WATER PIPES LEAKING

SOLUTION

	1	2	5	10
Remove old pipe and fix new copper pipe including all cutting and bending	85	120	225	400
Concrete or paving slabs surface	440	880	1760	1760
Tarmac surface	480	960	1920	1920
Clay paviors surface	530	1060	2120	2120

WATER PIPES BURST

SOLUTION

	1	2	5	10
Cut out and replace exposed copper pipework	105	155	–	–
Cut out and replace concealed copper pipework, behind access panel or the like	125	200	–	–

FITTINGS ARE FAULTY
Inspection recommends replacing/overhauling

SOLUTION

	Single Items £
Replace cold water storage cistern or tank and lid, 27l capacity	230
Replace cold water storage cistern or tank and lid, 44l capacity	400
Remove existing and install hot water cylinder size 1200 x 450mm and connect all pipework	350
Remove existing and install immersion heater	130

FITTINGS ARE FAULTY, CARRY OUT REPAIR

SOLUTION

Replace ball cock to cold water tank	115
Replace 32mm bottle trap and joints	66
Replace 40mm bottle trap and joints	83
Renew one 2-piece clip to copper pipe	55
Renew two 2-piece clips to copper pipe	60
Renew three 2-piece clips to copper pipe	65

	Suites £

FITTINGS ARE FAULTY
Inspection recommends replacing complete suites

SOLUTION
Rates for appliances include for standard range components, coloured white

Bathroom

Basin and pressed steel bath	**1130**
Basin and plastic bath	**1260**
Low level cistern WC with seat, basin and pressed steel bath	**1720**
Low level cistern WC with seat, basin and plastic bath	**1850**

Shower Room

Low level cistern WC with seat, basin and plastic shower tray	**1410**
Low level cistern WC with seat, basin and ceramic shower tray	**1530**

Cloakroom

Low level cistern WC with seat and basin	**1010**

Kitchen

Stainless steel sink with single bowl and drainer	**470**
Belfast sink	**580**

INDIVIDUAL FITTINGS ARE FAULTY
Inspection recommends replacing

SOLUTION
Rates for appliances include for standard range components,
coloured white

Replace fittings, complete with taps and waste and connecting all services

WC suite with low level cistern and seat	**555**
Wash basin	**415**
Belfast sink	**580**
Stainless steel sink with single bowl and drainer	**470**
Bath pressed steel	**715**
Bath plastic	**845**
Shower tray plastic	**405**
Shower tray ceramic	**530**
Toilet seat and cover	**105**

	Single Items £

INDIVIDUAL FITTINGS ARE FAULTY
Inspection recommends repair

SOLUTION

Shower tray, remove mastic and reseal perimeter	**75**
Replace shower head and bracket	**74**
Replace flexible shower hose	**70**
Renew ball valve including plastic float	**115**
Renew plastic syphonage unit to high or low level cisterns	**100**
Fit replacement washer to ball valve	**64**
Renew joint of WC to soil pipe with 102mm pan connector	**160**
Take off WC seat and cover provide new fixing kit and refix	**92**
Remove existing seat to WC pan and replace with new seat and cover	**105**
Refix loose sanitary fitting, rescrew brackets to wall	**83**
Fit replacement washer to tap	**64**
Replace faulty basin pillar tap with new to match existing	**105**
Replace faulty bib tap with new to match existing	**110**

BLOCKAGE IN FITTINGS

SOLUTION

Clear obstruction or blockage from bath, shower, basin, or sink, clean wastes and traps including removal and reassembling as necessary	**90**
Clear obstruction or blockage from WC pan, including cleaning and any necessary removal and reassembling	**100**

	RANGE	
	£	£

HEATING SYSTEM IS NOT WORKING
Inspection recommends replacement

SOLUTION
Replace heating system

Replace heating system excluding pipework
Wall mounted boiler, single and double panel radiators,
wall thermostat and programmer

	£		£
Clockwork programmer	**3620**	to	**5720**
Digital programmer	**4220**	to	**6320**

Replace heating system including pipework
Wall mounted boiler, single and double panel radiators,
pipework, wall thermostat and programmer

	£		£
Clockwork programmer	**5250**	to	**8610**
Digital programmer	**5850**	to	**9210**

Single
Items
£

INDIVIDUAL FITTINGS ARE FAULTY
Inspection recommends replacing or repairing

SOLUTION
Replace fittings

Replace boilers
Replace wall mounted boiler, including draining down system and
connecting to flue and pipework   **1410**
Replace free standing boiler, including draining down system and
connecting to flue and pipework   **3910**

Replace radiators including reconnection and rebalancing
Single panel 400 x 600mm   **150**
Single panel 500 x 1000mm   **190**
Single panel 600 x 1800mm   **295**
Double panel 400 x 500mm   **205**
Double panel 500 x 1200mm   **330**
Double panel 600 x 1600mm   **435**

Replace radiator valves
Replace radiator valves   **90**
Replace thermostatic radiator valve   **100**

Replace central heating controls
Cylinder thermostat   **77**
Wall thermostat   **80**
Programmer (clockwork)   **185**
Programmer (digital)   **785**

Cleaning out central heating system
Powerflush system   **355**

Repair storage heaters
Overhaul storage heaters, including inspecting fusible link, replace
thermostat, resetting thermal cutout and checking cable and testing **125**

2:3 FINISHES

INTERIOR
Ceilings

		RANGE	
		House Type	
	Terraced £		Detached £

CEILING IS BADLY DAMAGED OR COLLAPSED

SOLUTION
Replace ceiling

Apply plaster skim and decorate two coats
of emulsion paint

	Terraced £		Detached £
GROUND FLOOR	300	to	2130
FIRST FLOOR	370	to	2200
WHOLE HOUSE	670	to	4330

Replace lath and plaster or plasterboard
ceiling with plasterboard and apply two
coats of emulsion paint

	Terraced £		Detached £
GROUND FLOOR	720	to	5460
FIRST FLOOR	890	to	5640
WHOLE HOUSE	1610	to	11100

CEILING IS DAMAGED OR UNEVEN

SOLUTION
Construct an independent ceiling

Plasterboard on softwood battens and
decorate two coats of emulsion paint

	Terraced £		Detached £
GROUND FLOOR	690	to	4920
FIRST FLOOR	860	to	5090
WHOLE HOUSE	1550	to	10010

CEILING IS BADLY DAMAGED OR COLLAPSED

	Ceilings to Room Room Size		
	3 x 3m £	4 x 4m £	8 x 4m £

SOLUTION
Replace ceiling

	3 x 3m	4 x 4m	8 x 4m
Replace plasterboard ceiling and emulsion paint	380	675	1350
Replace lath and plaster ceiling and emulsion paint	405	720	1440

CEILING HAS SMALL CRACKS AND HOLES IN WHOLE AREA OF ROOM

SOLUTION
Repair ceiling

	3 x 3m	4 x 4m	8 x 4m
Apply plaster skim and decorate two coats emulsion paint	235	360	565

CEILING HAS SMALL CRACKS AND HOLES

SOLUTION
Repair ceiling

	Patches (number)			
	not exceeding 0.5m^2		not exceeding 1m^2	
	1 £	2 £	1 £	2 £
Replace plasterboard ceiling and emulsion paint	105	150	110	155
Replace lath and plaster ceiling and emulsion paint	110	160	145	225

	Length of Crack (m)			
	1 £	2 £	3 £	5 £
Rake out and fill in crack in plaster ceiling not exceeding 75mm wide	87	94	100	110

FLOOR COVERING IS DAMAGED

	Room Size m	RANGE Quality of Materials £		£

SOLUTION
Replace floor covering

	Room Size m	£		£
Carpet	3 x 3	535	to	690
	4 x 4	950	to	1230
	8 x 4	1900	to	2500
Carpet and underlay	3 x 3	605	to	760
	4 x 4	1070	to	1350
	8 x 4	2140	to	2700
PVC flooring, sheeting or tiles	3 x 3	495	to	580
	4 x 4	885	to	1030
	8 x 4	1770	to	2060
Quarry tiles	3 x 3	810		
	4 x 4	1440		
	8 x 4	2880		
Vitrified ceramic floor tiles	3 x 3	1120		
	4 x 4	1990		
	8 x 4	3990		
Wood flooring	3 x 3	555	to	810
	4 x 4	985	to	1440
	8 x 4	1970	to	2890

	Patches not exceeding 0.5m^2 (number			
	1 £	2 £	3 £	5 £

FLOOR COVERING IS DAMAGED IN SMALL AREAS

SOLUTION
Replace floor covering in damaged areas

	1	2	3	5
PVC floor tiles	63	76	89	115
Quarry tiles	130	215	300	405
Vitrified ceramic floor tiles	170	295	420	610
Wood strip flooring	83	115	150	215
Wood block flooring	97	145	190	285

	Skirtings to Room (one door opening) Room Size		
	3 x 3m	4 x 4m	8 x 4m
	£	£	£

SKIRTING IS DAMAGED OR MISSING

SOLUTION
Replace skirting

	3 x 3m	4 x 4m	8 x 4m
19 x 100mm chamfered and rounded softwood skirting, decorated	275	375	575
25 x 175mm torus section softwood skirting, decorated	295	400	610
Clay quarry tile coved skirting 150mm high	500	685	1050

SKIRTING IS LOOSE

SOLUTION
Refix loose skirtings

	3 x 3m	4 x 4m	8 x 4m
Resecure loose skirtings	89	105	130
Resecure loose skirtings and redecorate	175	220	315

	Skirting in Short Lengths		
	1m long	2m long	3m long
	£	£	£

SHORT LENGTHS OF SKIRTING ARE DAMAGED OR MISSING

SOLUTION
Replace skirting

	1m long	2m long	3m long
19 x 100mm chamfered and rounded softwood skirting, decorated	75	100	125
25 x 175mm torus section softwood skirting, decorated	77	105	130
Clay quarry tile coved skirting 150mm high	95	140	185

SHORT LENGTHS OF SKIRTING ARE LOOSE

SOLUTION
Refix loose skirtings

	1m long	2m long	3m long
Resecure loose skirtings	55	58	61
Resecure loose skirtings, repaint	61	73	84

		RANGE		
		Quality of Materials		
		£		£

WALL PLASTER IS LOOSE, CRACKED OR MISSING

SOLUTION

	Room Size (m)			
Rerender or replaster walls	3 x 3	1130	to	2190
	4 x 4	1550	to	3000
	8 x 4	2260	to	4390
Rerender or replaster walls including new skirting and decoration	3 x 3	1620	to	2670
	4 x 4	2210	to	3670
	8 x 4	3510	to	5870
Rerender or replaster walls	Walls 2.75m high			
	3m long	305	to	590
	4m long	420	to	815
	5m long	535	to	1040
	8m long	840	to	1630
Rerender or replaster walls including new skirting and decoration	3m long	440	to	725
	4m long	600	to	990
	5m long	760	to	1260
	8m long	1200	to	1980

PATCHES OF WALL PLASTER ARE LOOSE, CRACKED OR MISSING

SOLUTION
Replaster patches in wall plaster

	Number of Patches (number)			
Small patches not exceeding 0.5m2 in area	1	85	to	100
	2	135	to	150
	3	175	to	200
	5	255	to	300
Small patches not exceeding 1m2 in area	1	110	to	145
	2	170	to	240
	3	230	to	335
	5	350	to	525

CRACKS IN PLASTER

SOLUTION

Repair cracks

	Length of Crack (m)			
	1	2	3	5
	£	£	£	£
Rake out and refill crack in plaster	**56**	**63**	**70**	**82**

	Number of Cracks (number)			
	1	2	3	5
	£	£	£	£
Rake out and refill crack in plaster 1m long	**56**	**62**	**68**	**78**

	RANGE		
	Quality of Materials		
	£		£

WALL TILING IN POOR CONDITION, TILES MISSING

SOLUTION
Replace wall tiles

	Tiles (m²)			
600mm high to splashbacks 1m long	0.6	**95**	to	**100**
600mm high to splashbacks 1m long	1.2	**140**	to	**150**
600mm high to splashbacks 1m long	1.8	**190**	to	**200**
600mm high to splashbacks 1m long	3	**280**	to	**305**
Walls 2.75m high, 2m long	5.5	**425**	to	**465**
Walls 2.75m high, 3m long	8	**615**	to	**680**
Walls 2.75m high, 4m long	11	**845**	to	**935**
Walls 2.75m high, 5m long	14	**1080**	to	**1190**
1.2m high to bathrooms	11	**845**	to	**935**
Full height to showers	10	**770**	to	**850**
Full height to bathrooms	25	**1920**	to	**2120**

PATCHES OF WALL TILING IN POOR CONDITION, TILES MISSING

SOLUTION
Replace wall tiles in small areas

Patches not exceeding 0.5m² area

Number of Patches			
1	**120**	to	**165**
2	**140**	to	**150**
3	**190**	to	**200**
5	**280**	to	**305**

Patches not exceeding 1.0m² area

1	**155**	to	**165**
2	**260**	to	**280**
3	**365**	to	**395**
5	**530**	to	**575**

	Height of Cladding (m)	Length of Cladding (m)		
		3 £	5 £	8 £

VERTICAL CLADDING IS IN POOR DECORATIVE ORDER

SOLUTION
Prepare and redecorate timber cladding at low level
Clean down, one undercoat, one finishing coat oil paint

	1.2	**100**	**135**	**185**
	3.0	**220**	**300**	**390**

Clean down, one coat polyurethane varnish

	1.2	**84**	**105**	**140**
	3.0	**160**	**220**	**270**

Clean down, one coat woodstain system

	1.2	**115**	**155**	**215**
	3.0	**260**	**360**	**470**

Rub down, prepare and paint one coat knotting and primer, two undercoats, one finishing coat oil paint

	1.2	**140**	**200**	**290**
	3.0	**350**	**500**	**600**

Burn off paint, prepare and paint one coat knotting and primer, two undercoats, one finishing coat oil paint

	1.2	**180**	**265**	**395**
	3.0	**430**	**630**	**860**

	Height of Cladding (m)	Length of Cladding (m)		
		3 £	5 £	8 £

VERTICAL CLADDING IS IN POOR DECORATIVE ORDER

SOLUTION
Prepare and redecorate timber cladding at high level
Clean down, one undercoat, one finishing coat oil paint

	1.2	135	170	240
	3.0	305	385	465
	6.0	460	700	900

Clean down, one coat polyurethane varnish

	1.2	120	140	195
	3.0	245	305	365
	6.0	380	580	725

Clean down, one coat woodstain system

	1.2	150	190	270
	3.0	340	440	540
	6.0	510	785	1020

Rub down, prepare and paint one coat knotting and primer, two undercoats, one finishing coat oil paint

	1.2	175	235	345
	3.0	435	585	715
	6.0	645	990	1310

Burn off paint, prepare and paint one coat knotting and primer, two undercoats, one finishing coat oil paint

	1.2	215	300	450
	3.0	490	735	975
	6.0	830	1280	1720

	Doors	
	One Side	Both Sides
	£	£

DOORS ARE IN POOR DECORATIVE ORDER

SOLUTION
Prepare and redecorate doors

Clean down, one undercoat, one finishing coat oil paint

	One Side	Both Sides
flush or half glazed	77	105
fully glazed	69	86

Clean down, one coat polyurethane varnish

	One Side	Both Sides
flush or half glazed	67	84
fully glazed	64	77

Clean down, one coat woodstain system

	One Side	Both Sides
flush or half glazed	81	115
fully glazed	66	81

Rub down, prepare and paint one coat knotting and primer, two undercoats, one finishing coat oil paint

	One Side	Both Sides
flush or half glazed	105	160
fully glazed	75	99

Burn off paint, prepare and paint one coat knotting and primer, two undercoats, one finishing coat oil paint

	One Side	Both Sides
flush or half glazed	135	225
fully glazed	130	210

	Door Frames	
	One Side	Both Sides
	£	£

DOOR FRAMES ARE IN POOR DECORATIVE ORDER

SOLUTION
Prepare and redecorate door frames

	One Side	Both Sides
Clean down, one undercoat, one finishing coat oil paint	94	140
Clean down, one coat polyurethane varnish	78	105
Clean down, one coat woodstain system	115	150
Rub down, prepare and paint one coat knotting and primer, two undercoats, one finishing coat oil paint	140	230
Burn off paint, prepare and paint one coat knotting and primer, two undercoats, one finishing coat oil paint	195	340

	Door and Frame			
	Without Fanlight		With Fanlight	
	One Side	Both Sides	One Side	Both Sides
	£	£	£	£

DOORS AND FRAMES ARE IN POOR DECORATIVE ORDER

SOLUTION
Prepare and redecorate doors

Clean down, one undercoat, one finishing coat oil paint

flush or half glazed doors	130	205	150	240
fully glazed doors	125	185	140	225

Clean down, one coat polyurethane varnish

flush or half glazed doors	100	145	115	160
fully glazed doors	97	140	110	160

Clean down, one coat woodstain system

flush or half glazed doors	135	220	155	255
fully glazed doors	120	185	140	225

Rub down, prepare and paint one coat knotting and primer, two undercoats, one finishing coat oil paint

flush or half glazed doors	210	355	245	425
fully glazed doors	180	295	215	365

Burn off paint, prepare and paint one coat knotting and primer, two undercoats, one finishing coat oil paint

flush or half glazed doors	310	540	370	655
fully glazed doors	300	525	355	640

	RANGE		
	Approx Window Size (mm)		
	600 x 900 £	to	1500 x 1200 £

WINDOWS ARE IN POOR DECORATIVE ORDER

SOLUTION
Prepare and redecorate windows

Low level

Clean down, one undercoat, one finishing coat oil paint	63	to	105
Clean down, one coat polyurethane varnish	61	to	94
Clean down, one coat woodstain system	63	to	105
Rub down, prepare and paint one coat knotting and primer, two undercoats, one finishing coat oil paint	69	to	160
Burn off paint, prepare and paint one coat knotting and primer, two undercoats, one finishing coat oil paint	70	to	165

High level

Clean down, one undercoat, one finishing coat oil paint	88	to	135
Clean down, one coat polyurethane varnish	85	to	115
Clean down, one coat woodstain system	88	to	125
Rub down, prepare and paint one coat knotting and primer, two undercoats, one finishing coat oil paint	120	to	205
Burn off paint, prepare and paint one coat knotting and primer, two undercoats, one finishing coat oil paint	125	to	210

WINDOWS ARE IN POOR DECORATIVE ORDER	Per Elevation - Window Sizes			
	Example A £	Example B £	Example C £	Example D £

SOLUTION
Prepare and redecorate windows

Clean down, one undercoat, one finishing coat oil paint

Windows with one pane	185	230	245	255
Windows with two or more panes	200	230	250	255
Georgian type windows with small panes	295	385	440	465

Clean down, one coat polyurethane varnish

Windows with one pane	175	215	230	235
Windows with two or more panes	185	230	250	255
Georgian type windows with small panes	240	305	335	355

Clean down, one coat woodstain system

Windows with one pane	175	215	230	235
Windows with two or more panes	200	250	275	285
Georgian type windows with small panes	270	350	395	420

Rub down, prepare and paint one coat knotting and primer, two undercoats, one finishing coat oil paint

Windows with one pane	250	315	345	380
Windows with two or more panes	275	355	400	430
Georgian type windows with small panes	405	550	685	710

Burn off paint, prepare and paint one coat knotting and primer, two undercoats, one finishing coat oil paint

Windows with one pane	260	330	360	400
Windows with two or more panes	295	385	435	460
Georgian type windows with small panes	470	660	785	830

Number and sizes of windows in tables above

Example A	two 1500 x 1200mm, one 1200 x 1200mm
Example B	four 1500 x 1200mm, one 900 x 900mm
Example C	one 1800 x 1800mm, two 1500 x 1200mm one 1200 x 1200mm, one 1200 x 900mm
Example D	one 1800 x 1800mm, four 1500 x 1200mm

	RANGE House Type		
	Terraced £		Detached £

WINDOWS ARE IN POOR DECORATIVE ORDER

SOLUTION
Prepare and redecorate windows

Clean down, one undercoat, one finishing coat oil paint

Windows with one pane	225	to	999
Windows with two or more panes	258	to	1143
Georgian type windows with small panes	446	to	2213

Clean down, one coat polyurethane varnish

Windows with one pane	202	to	875
Windows with two or more panes	228	to	1005
Georgian type windows with small panes	323	to	1540

Clean down, one coat woodstain system

Windows with one pane	205	to	877
Windows with two or more panes	256	to	1139
Georgian type windows with small panes	388	to	1891

Rub down, prepare and paint one coat knotting and primer, two undercoats, one finishing coat oil paint

Windows with one pane	294	to	1355
Windows with two or more panes	358	to	1712
Georgian type windows with small panes	595	to	3015

Burn off paint, prepare and paint one coat knotting and primer, two undercoats, one finishing coat oil paint

Windows with one pane	328	to	1542
Windows with two or more panes	412	to	1923
Georgian type windows with small panes	743	to	3815

	RANGE House Type		
	Terraced £		Detached £

WINDOWS, DOORS AND FRAMES ARE IN POOR DECORATIVE ORDER

SOLUTION
Prepare and redecorate windows, doors and frames

Clean down, one undercoat, one finishing coat oil paint

Windows with one pane	385	to	1159
Windows with two or more panes	418	to	1303
Georgian type windows with small panes	606	to	2373

Clean down, one coat polyurethane varnish

Windows with one pane	302	to	975
Windows with two or more panes	328	to	1105
Georgian type windows with small panes	423	to	1640

Clean down, one coat woodstain system

Windows with one pane	375	to	1047
Windows with two or more panes	426	to	1309
Georgian type windows with small panes	558	to	2061

Rub down, prepare and paint one coat knotting and primer, two undercoats, one finishing coat oil paint

Windows with one pane	614	to	1675
Windows with two or more panes	678	to	2032
Georgian type windows with small panes	915	to	3335

Burn off paint, prepare and paint one coat knotting and primer, two undercoats, one finishing coat oil paint

Windows with one pane	848	to	2062
Windows with two or more panes	932	to	2443
Georgian type windows with small panes	1263	to	4335

CEILING IS BADLY STAINED/IN POOR DECORATIVE ORDER

SOLUTION
Redecorate ceiling

	RANGE House Type		
	Terraced £		Detached £
Ceiling decoration to whole house			
Lining paper and emulsion paint	795	to	5150
Embossed paper and emulsion paint	890	to	5770
Emulsion paint	240	to	1620
Ceiling decoration to ground floor			
Lining paper and emulsion paint	355	to	2530
Embossed paper and emulsion paint	400	to	2840
Emulsion paint	160	to	795
Ceiling decoration to first floor			
Lining paper and emulsion paint	440	to	2620
Embossed paper and emulsion pain.	495	to	2930
Emulsion paint	190	to	820

	Ceilings to Room Room Size		
	3 x 3m £	4 x 4m £	8 x 4m £
Emulsion paint to existing painted ceilings	110	165	270
Emulsion paint to existing artex ceilings	160	260	455
Remove expanded polystyrene tiles, prepare and apply emulsion paint to ceiling	230	315	635
Replace paper			
Hang lining paper and emulsion paint	175	335	670
Hang embossed paper and emulsion paint	200	375	750

	Ceilings to Room Room Size		
	3 x 3m £	4 x 4m £	8 x 4m £

EXPANDED POLYSTYRENE TILES
MISSING AND LOOSE

SOLUTION
Remove expanded polystyrene tiles

	3 x 3m	4 x 4m	8 x 4m
Prepare and apply emulsion paint to ceiling	230	315	635
Hang lining paper and emulsion paint	275	505	1010
Hang embossed paper and emulsion paint	315	545	1090

	Floors to Room Room Size		
	3 x 3m £	4 x 4m £	8 x 4m £

FLOOR IS BADLY STAINED/IN POOR
DECORATIVE ORDER

SOLUTION
Redecorate flooring

	3 x 3m	4 x 4m	8 x 4m
Two coats matt finish polyurethane varnish to timber floors	250	410	720
Two coats non slip paint to concrete floors	250	410	720

	Rooms (wall height 2.75m)		
	Room Size		
	3 x 3m	4 x 4m	8 x 4m
	3 x 3m	4 x 4m	8 x 4m
	1 door	1 door	2 doors
	1 Window	1 Window	2 Windows
	Size 1200 x	Size 1200 x	Sizes
	1200mm	1200mm	900 x
			1200mm and
			1800 x
			1800mm
	£	£	£

WALLS ARE BADLY STAINED/IN POOR DECORATIVE ORDER

SOLUTION
Clean existing walls

Remove mould from wall with fungicidal wash	**315**	**350**	**510**

Repaper walls

Hang woodchip or embossed paper and decorate	**510**	**705**	**1030**
Hang vinyl paper (PC £8 per roll)	**680**	**930**	**1360**

Two coats emulsion paint

To existing painted and new plastered walls	**265**	**340**	**405**
To embossed paper or similar	**325**	**360**	**525**

Wash and clean down walls and apply two coats oil paint

To prepared plastered or embossed papered walls	**320**	**435**	**635**

	Walls 2.75m high			
	3m long	4m long	5m long	8m long
	m²	m²	m²	m²
	8	11	14	22
	£	£	£	£

WALLS ARE BADLY STAINED/IN POOR DECORATIVE ORDER

SOLUTION
Clean existing walls

	3m long	4m long	5m long	8m long
Remove mould from wall with fungicidal wash	120	145	170	240
Repaper walls				
Hang woodchip or embossed paper	155	190	230	335
Hang woodchip or embossed paper and decorate	220	280	345	450
Hang vinyl paper (PC £8 per roll)	235	315	370	490
Two coats emulsion paint				
To existing painted and new plastered walls	105	125	145	200
To embossed paper or similar	120	145	175	245
Wash and clean down walls and apply two coats oil paint				
To prepared plastered or embossed papered walls	135	165	200	285

**DOORS ARE IN POOR
DECORATIVE ORDER**

SOLUTION
Prepare and redecorate doors

	Doors		Frames	
	One Side	Both Sides	One Side	Both Sides
	£	£	£	£
Clean down, one undercoat, one finishing coat oil paint	78	105	81	97
Clean down, one coat polyurethane varnish	65	80	75	90
Clean down, one coat woodstain system	84	120	105	120
Rub down, prepare and paint one coat knotting and primer, two undercoats, one finishing coat oil paint	100	150	105	135
Burn off paint, prepare and paint one coat knotting and primer, two undercoats, one finishing coat oil paint	120	195	135	175

	Door and Frame			
	Without Fanlight		With Fanlight	
	One Side	Both Sides	One Side	Both Sides
	£	£	£	£
Clean down, one undercoat, one finishing coat oil paint	110	155	120	170
Clean down, one coat polyurethane varnish	100	110	115	155
Clean down, one coat woodstain system	140	150	160	220
Rub down, prepare and paint one coat knotting and primer, two undercoats, one finishing coat oil paint	155	235	175	270
Burn off paint, prepare and paint one coat knotting and primer, two undercoats, one finishing coat oil paint	210	320	245	370

	Doors (number)			
	7 £	10 £	12 £	13 £

DOORS ARE IN POOR DECORATIVE ORDER

SOLUTION
Prepare and redecorate doors one side

Clean down, one undercoat, one finishing coat oil paint	245	270	325	355
Clean down, one coat polyurethane varnish	180	240	275	295
Clean down, one coat woodstain system	290	345	415	450
Rub down, prepare and paint one coat knotting and primer, two undercoats, one finishing coat oil paint	350	500	600	650
Burn off paint, prepare and paint one coat knotting and primer, two undercoats, one finishing coat oil paint	505	720	865	935

Prepare and redecorate doors both sides

Clean down, one undercoat, one finishing coat oil paint	395	565	675	735
Clean down, one coat polyurethane varnish	265	375	450	490
Clean down, one coat woodstain system	480	690	825	895
Rub down, prepare and paint one coat knotting and primer, two undercoats, one finishing coat oil paint	700	1000	1200	1300
Burn off paint, prepare and paint one coat knotting and primer, two undercoats, one finishing coat oil paint	1010	1440	1730	1870

	Doors (number)			
	7	10	12	13
	£	£	£	£

DOOR FRAMES ARE IN POOR DECORATIVE ORDER

SOLUTION
Prepare and redecorate door frames one side

	7	10	12	13
Clean down, one undercoat, one finishing coat oil paint	220	315	375	405
Clean down, one coat polyurethane varnish	220	315	375	405
Clean down, one coat woodstain system	385	550	655	710
Rub down, prepare and paint one coat knotting and primer, two undercoats, one finishing coat oil paint	385	550	655	710
Burn off paint, prepare and paint one coat knotting and primer, two undercoats, one finishing coat oil paint	605	860	1030	1120

Prepare and redecorate door frames both sides

	7	10	12	13
Clean down, one undercoat, one finishing coat oil paint	330	470	565	610
Clean down, one coat polyurethane varnish	330	470	565	610
Clean down, one coat woodstain system	495	705	845	915
Rub down, prepare and paint one coat knotting and primer, two undercoats, one finishing coat oil paint	605	860	1030	1120
Burn off paint, prepare and paint one coat knotting and primer, two undercoats, one finishing coat oil paint	875	1250	1500	1630

	Doors and Frames (number)			
	7 £	10 £	12 £	13 £
		(without fanlights)		

DOOR AND FRAMES ARE IN POOR DECORATIVE ORDER

SOLUTION

Prepare and redecorate door and frames, one side

	7	10	12	13
Clean down, one undercoat, one finishing coat oil paint	415	595	715	775
Clean down, one coat polyurethane varnish	350	500	600	650
Clean down, one coat woodstain system	625	890	1070	1220
Rub down, prepare and paint one coat knotting and primer, two undercoats, one finishing coat oil paint	735	1050	1260	1360
Burn off paint, prepare and paint one coat knotting and primer, two undercoats, one finishing coat oil paint	1110	1580	1900	2060

Prepare and redecorate door and frames, both sides

	7	10	12	13
Clean down, one undercoat, one finishing coat oil paint	725	1030	1240	1340
Clean down, one coat polyurethane varnish	590	845	1010	1100
Clean down, one coat woodstain system	975	1390	1670	1810
Rub down, prepare and paint one coat knotting and primer, two undercoats, one finishing coat oil paint	1300	1860	2230	2420
Burn off paint, prepare and paint one coat knotting and primer, two undercoats, one finishing coat oil paint	1880	2690	3230	3500

	Doors and Frames (number)		
7	10	12	13
£	£	£	£
	(with fanlights)		

DOOR AND FRAMES ARE IN POOR DECORATIVE ORDER

SOLUTION
Prepare and redecorate door and frames, one side

	7	10	12	13
Clean down, one undercoat, one finishing coat oil paint	505	720	865	935
Clean down, one coat polyurethane varnish	440	625	750	815
Clean down, one coat woodstain system	780	1110	1330	1440
Rub down, prepare and paint one coat knotting and primer, two undercoats, one finishing coat oil paint	890	1270	1520	1650
Burn off paint, prepare and paint one coat knotting and primer, two undercoats, one finishing coat oil paint	1350	1920	2310	2500

Prepare and redecorate door and frames, both sides

	7	10	12	13
Clean down, one undercoat, one finishing coat oil paint	855	1220	1460	1590
Clean down, one coat polyurethane varnish	725	1030	1240	1340
Clean down, one coat woodstain system	1170	1670	2010	2180
Rub down, prepare and paint one coat knotting and primer, two undercoats, one finishing coat oil paint	1540	2210	2650	2870
Burn off paint, prepare and paint one coat knotting and primer, two undercoats, one finishing coat oil paint	2230	3190	3830	4150

	RANGE Approx Window Size (mm)		
	600 x 900 £		1500 x 1200 £

WINDOWS ARE IN POOR DECORATIVE ORDER

SOLUTION
Prepare and redecorate windows

Clean down, one undercoat, one finishing coat oil paint

Windows with one pane	63	to	77
Windows with two or more panes	66	to	81
Georgian type windows with small panes	72	to	105

Clean down, one coat polyurethane varnish

Windows with one pane	61	to	73
Windows with two or more panes	63	to	77
Georgian type windows with small panes	66	to	94

Clean down, one coat woodstain system

Windows with one pane	63	to	73
Windows with two or more panes	66	to	81
Georgian type windows with small panes	72	to	105

Rub down, prepare and paint one coat knotting and primer, two undercoats, one finishing coat oil paint

Windows with one pane	69	to	91
Windows with two or more panes	75	to	99
Georgian type windows with small panes	86	to	160

Burn off paint, prepare and paint one coat knotting and primer, two undercoats, one finishing coat oil paint

Windows with one pane	70	to	94
Windows with two or more panes	78	to	105
Georgian type windows with small panes	88	to	165

SKIRTINGS ARE IN POOR DECORATIVE ORDER

	Skirting to Room (with one door opening) Room Size		
	3 x 3m £	4 x 4m £	8 x 4m £

SOLUTION
Prepare and redecorate skirtings

Clean down, one undercoat, one finishing coat oil paint	135	160	200

	Skirting in Short Lengths		
	1m long £	2m long £	3m long £
Clean down, one undercoat, one finishing coat oil paint	73	79	85

	Wall String	Straight Flight Staircase		
		Handrail	Balusters Posts & Base	Handrail etc Complete
	£	£	£	£

STAIRCASES ARE IN POOR DECORATIVE ORDER

SOLUTION
Prepare and redecorate staircases

	Wall String	Handrail	Balusters Posts & Base	Handrail etc Complete
Clean down, prepare and apply paint to wood surfaces				
One undercoat and one finishing coat oil paint	77	91	185	250
One coat polyurethane varnish	77	70	155	200
One coat woodstain system	97	77	220	295
One undercoat and one finishing coat oil paint to balusters and one coat polyurethane varnish to handrails	77	70	185	230
One undercoat and one finishing coat oil paint to balusters and one coat woodstain to handrails	77	77	185	240
Rub down surfaces and apply paint to wood surfaces				
One coat knotting and primer, two undercoats and one finishing coat oil paint	97	125	290	410
One coat knotting and primer, two undercoats and one finishing coat oil paint to balusters and one coat polyurethane varnish to handrails	97	70	210	280
One coat knotting and primer, two undercoats and one finishing coat oil paint to balusters and one coat woodstain to handrails	125	77	335	435
Burn off, prepare and apply paint to wood surfaces				
One coat knotting and primer, two undercoats and one finishing coat oil paint	125	160	335	520
One coat knotting and primer, two undercoats and one finishing coat oil paint to balusters and one coat polyurethane varnish to handrails	125	70	335	430
One coat knotting and primer, two undercoats and one finishing coat oil paint to balusters and one coat woodstain to handrails	97	77	210	285

RENDERED BOUNDARY WALL IS IN POOR DECORATIVE ORDER

SOLUTION
Redecorate boundary wall

	Length of Wall (m)			
	1	5	10	20
	£	£	£	£
One coat exterior cement paint or water compound or exterior Sandtex matt paint				
1m high	62	110	165	280
1.5m high	68	140	225	350
2m high	73	165	285	470

FENCES ARE IN POOR DECORATIVE ORDER

	Length of fence (m)			
SOLUTION	1	5	10	20
Redecorate fences	£	£	£	£
Prepare timber and apply two coats of external quality wood treatment				
1m high open boarded fencing	77	185	320	545
2m high open boarded fencing	105	320	545	1090
1m high close boarded fencing	74	170	290	480
2m high close boarded fencing	98	290	480	960
Prepare timber and apply two coats of polyurethane varnish				
1m high open boarded fencing	70	150	250	400
2m high open boarded fencing	90	250	400	800
1m high close boarded fencing	68	140	235	365
2m high close boarded fencing	87	235	365	730
Prepare timber and apply two coats of exterior quality gloss paint				
1m high open boarded fencing	69	145	240	375
2m high open boarded fencing	88	240	375	755
1m high close boarded fencing	67	135	225	345
2m high close boarded fencing	85	225	345	695
Prepare metal surfaces and apply one coat primer and one coat gloss paint				
1m high open boarded fencing	69	145	240	380
2m high open boarded fencing	88	240	380	760
1m high close boarded fencing	68	140	230	360
2m high close boarded fencing	86	230	360	720

GATES ARE IN POOR DECORATIVE ORDER

SOLUTION
Redecorate gates

	Gate Size		
	900 x 700mm £	800 x 2000mm £	900 x 2400mm £
Prepare timber and apply two coats of external quality wood treatment			
Open boarded gates	85	135	170
Close boarded gates	80	125	155
Prepare timber and apply two coats of polyurethane varnish			
Open boarded gates	75	115	150
Close boarded gates	74	110	130
Prepare timber and apply two coats of exterior quality gloss paint			
Open boarded gates	74	110	130
Close boarded gates	72	105	140
Prepare metal surfaces and apply one coat primer and one coat gloss paint			
Open boarded gates	74	110	130
Close boarded gates	74	110	130

	Height of Cladding (m)	Length of Cladding (m)		
		3 £	5 £	8 £

VERTICAL CLADDING IS IN POOR DECORATIVE ORDER

SOLUTION
Prepare and redecorate timber cladding

	Height of Cladding (m)	3 £	5 £	8 £
Clean down, one undercoat, one finishing coat oil paint	1.2	100	135	185
	3.0	220	300	390
Clean down, one coat polyurethane varnish	1.2	84	105	140
	3.0	160	220	270
Clean down, one coat woodstain system	1.2	115	155	215
	3.0	260	360	470
Rub down, prepare and paint one coat knotting and primer, two undercoats, one finishing coat oil paint	1.2	140	200	290
	3.0	350	500	600
Burn off paint, prepare and paint one coat knotting and primer, two undercoats, one finishing coat oil paint	1.2	180	265	395
	3.0	430	630	860

DOORS ARE IN POOR DECORATIVE ORDER

SOLUTION
Prepare and redecorate doors

	Doors	
	One Side	Both Sides
	£	£
Clean down, one undercoat, one finishing coat oil paint		
flush or half glazed	77	105
fully glazed	69	86
Clean down, one coat polyurethane varnish		
flush or half glazed	67	84
fully glazed	64	77
Clean down, one coat woodstain system		
flush or half glazed	81	115
fully glazed	66	81
Rub down, prepare and paint one coat knotting and primer, two undercoats, one finishing coat oil paint		
flush or half glazed	105	160
fully glazed	75	99
Burn off paint, prepare and paint one coat knotting and primer, two undercoats, one finishing coat oil paint		
flush or half glazed	135	225
fully glazed	130	210

DOOR FRAMES ARE IN POOR DECORATIVE ORDER

SOLUTION

	Door Frames	
	One Side	Both Sides
	£	£
Prepare and redecorate door frames		
Clean down, one undercoat, one finishing coat oil paint	94	140
Clean down, one coat polyurethane varnish	78	105
Clean down, one coat woodstain system	115	150
Rub down, prepare and paint one coat knotting and primer, two undercoats, one finishing coat oil paint	140	230
Burn off paint, prepare and paint one coat knotting and primer, two undercoats, one finishing coat oil paint	195	340

	Door and Frame			
	Without Fanlight		With Fanlight	
	One Side	Both Sides	One Side	Both Sides
	£	£	£	£

**DOORS AND FRAMES ARE IN POOR
DECORATIVE ORDER**

SOLUTION
Prepare and redecorate doors
Clean down, one undercoat, one finishing coat
oil paint

flush or half glazed doors	130	205	150	240
fully glazed doors	125	185	140	225

Clean down, one coat polyurethane varnish

flush or half glazed doors	100	145	115	160
fully glazed doors	97	140	110	160

Clean down, one coat woodstain system

flush or half glazed doors	135	220	155	255
fully glazed doors	120	185	140	225

Rub down, prepare and paint one coat knotting
and primer, two undercoats, one finishing coat
oil paint

flush or half glazed doors	210	355	245	425
fully glazed doors	180	295	215	365

Burn off paint, prepare and paint one coat
knotting and primer, two undercoats, one
finishing coat oil paint

flush or half glazed doors	310	540	370	655
fully glazed doors	300	525	355	640

	RANGE	
	Approximate Window Size	
	600 x 900mm	1500 x 1200mm
	£	£

WINDOWS ARE IN POOR DECORATIVE ORDER

SOLUTION
Prepare and redecorate windows

	One Side		
Clean down, one undercoat, one finishing coat oil paint	**63**	to	**105**
Clean down, one coat polyurethane varnish	**61**	to	**94**
Clean down, one coat woodstain system	**63**	to	**105**
Rub down, prepare and paint one coat knotting and primer, two undercoats, one finishing coat oil paint	**69**	to	**160**
Burn off paint, prepare and paint one coat knotting and primer, two undercoats, one finishing coat oil paint	**70**	to	**165**
	Both Sides		
Clean down, one undercoat, one finishing coat oil paint	**75**	to	**175**
Clean down, one coat polyurethane varnish	**72**	to	**140**
Clean down, one coat woodstain system	**75**	to	**160**
Rub down, prepare and paint one coat knotting and primer, two undercoats, one finishing coat oil paint	**88**	to	**265**
Burn off paint, prepare and paint one coat knotting and primer, two undercoats, one finishing coat oil paint	**91**	to	**280**

2:5 COMMON ALTERATION WORKS

EXTERIOR
Roof Coverings

	RANGE House Type		
	Terraced £		Detached £
Replace roof covering including battens and felt			
Plain clay, concrete tiles	**3130**	to	**23940**
Concrete interlocking tiles	**2030**	to	**14870**
Clay pantiles	**2190**	to	**18460**
Welsh blue natural slates	**5790**	to	**40840**
Westmorland green natural slates	**10480**	to	**86380**
Reconstructed stone slates	**5160**	to	**33170**
Fibre cement slates	**5480**	to	**30830**
Concrete interlocking slates	**4690**	to	**31450**

	RANGE House Type		
	Terraced £		Detached £

Replace boarding to roof

Replace softwood boarding

Replace eaves fascia and soffit, including decoration

	Terraced £		Detached £
ONE ELEVATION	380	to	1260
WHOLE HOUSE	760	to	4040

Replace eaves fascia, including decoration

ONE ELEVATION	215	to	655
WHOLE HOUSE	430	to	2120

Replace eaves soffit, including decoration

ONE ELEVATION	220	to	655
WHOLE HOUSE	440	to	2120

Replace PVCu boarding

Replace white eaves fascia and soffit

ONE ELEVATION	405	to	1110
WHOLE HOUSE	810	to	3430

Replace white eaves fascia

ONE ELEVATION	205	to	580
WHOLE HOUSE	410	to	1830

Replace white eaves soffit

ONE ELEVATION	505	to	1410
WHOLE HOUSE	1010	to	4510

Replace mahogany eaves fascia and soffit

ONE ELEVATION	505	to	1410
WHOLE HOUSE	1010	to	4510

Replace mahogany eaves fascia

ONE ELEVATION	285	to	825
WHOLE HOUSE	570	to	2600

Replace mahogany eaves soffit

ONE ELEVATION	220	to	640
WHOLE HOUSE	440	to	2020

Replace boarding to roof

Replace softwood boarding

Replace verges, including decoration

ONE SIDE ELEVATION				
One Side	**290**	to	**505**
Both sides	**580**	to	**1010**
TWO ELEVATIONS	**1000**	to	**1640**

Replace PVCu boarding

Replace verges with white PVCu

ONE SIDE ELEVATION				
One Side	**375**	to	**535**
Both sides	**750**	to	**1070**
TWO ELEVATIONS	**1280**	to	**2140**

Replace verges with mahogany PVCu

ONE SIDE ELEVATION				
One Side	**425**	to	**605**
Both sides	**830**	to	**1210**
TWO ELEVATIONS	**1440**	to	**2420**

	House Type		
	Terraced £		Detached £

Replace gutters and downpipes

PVCu

ONE ELEVATION	**330**	to	**580**
WHOLE HOUSE	**685**	to	**2050**

Metal

ONE ELEVATION	**485**	to	**1350**
WHOLE HOUSE	**995**	to	**4720**

	RANGE		
	House Type		
	Terraced £		Detached £

Replace windows

Take out and install double glazed windows

	Terraced £		Detached £
PVCu casement window	3125	to	17325
PVCu sash window	9550	to	50990

Take out and install windows including single glazing
and decorating externally

Timber casement window	2645	to	13670
Metal casement window	3185	to	16690
Timber double hung sash window	5555	to	29275

Take out and install windows including double glazing
and decorating externally

Timber casement window	3835	to	19720
Metal casement window	4170	to	21235
Timber double hung sash window	6460	to	33870

Replace windows and doors

Take out and install double glazed windows and doors

PVCu casement window	4645	to	18845
PVCu sash window	11070	to	52510

Take out and install windows and doors
including single glazing and decorating externally

Timber casement window	4075	to	15350
Metal casement window	4615	to	18370
Timber double hung sash window	6985	to	30955

Take out and install windows and doors
including double glazing and decorating externally

Timber casement window	5265	to	21400
Metal casement window	5600	to	22915
Timber double hung sash window	7890	to	35550

	Opening Width		
	3m	4m	5m
	£	£	£
Form opening between rooms and make good (excluding floor finish)			
Form opening in non structural wall	380	460	540
Form opening in structural wall including providing steel beam over opening	750	950	1150

	Terraced £	RANGE House Type	Detached £

Independent ceiling

Plasterboard on softwood battens and decorate
two coats of emulsion paint

	Terraced £		Detached £
GROUND FLOOR	**690**	to	**4920**
FIRST FLOOR	**860**	to	**5090**
WHOLE HOUSE	**1550**	to	**10010**

		RANGE House Type		
		Terraced £		Detached £
Timber floors				
Replace flooring				
Softwood floor boards				
GROUND FLOOR		**1270**	to	**8240**
FIRST FLOOR		**1030**	to	**7970**
WHOLE HOUSE		**2300**	to	**16210**

	Room Size	RANGE Quality of Materials		
	m	£		£
Replace floor covering				
Carpet				
	3 x 3	**535**	to	**690**
	4 x 4	**950**	to	**1230**
	8 x 4	**1900**	to	**2500**
Carpet and underlay				
	3 x 3	**605**	to	**760**
	4 x 4	**1070**	to	**1350**
	8 x 4	**2140**	to	**2700**
PVC flooring, sheeting or tiles				
	3 x 3	**495**	to	**580**
	4 x 4	**885**	to	**1030**
	8 x 4	**1770**	to	**2060**
Quarry tiles				
	3 x 3	**810**		
	4 x 4	**1440**		
	8 x 4	**2880**		
Vitrified ceramic floor tiles				
	3 x 3	**1120**		
	4 x 4	**1990**		
	8 x 4	**3990**		
Wood flooring				
	3 x 3	**555**	to	**810**
	4 x 4	**985**	to	**1440**
	8 x 4	**1970**	to	**2890**

	BATHROOM			SHOWER CUBICLE
		Tiling to		
	FULL HEIGHT	1200mm HIGH	600mm HIGH	FULL HEIGHT
	Area of Tiling			
	25m^2	11m^2	2m^2	10m^2
	£	£	£	£

Wall Tiling

Replace tiling

White glazed ceramic wall tiles	**1920**	**845**	**190**	**770**
Light coloured glazed ceramic wall tiles	**2050**	**905**	**205**	**820**
Dark coloured glazed ceramic wall tiles	**2120**	**935**	**220**	**850**

Bathroom size 2.5 x 2.5m x 2.75m high with one
door and one window size 600 x 600mm
Shower size 1.2 x 1.2 x 2.75m high with one door

	Single Items £
Fireplaces	
Replace pine mantle	**325**
Replace micro marble mantle	**800**
Replace hearth with Decostone	**325**
Replace hearth with conglomerate marble	**380**
Replace with conglomerate marble back panel and hearth, pine mantle	**610**
Replace with green marble or black granite back panel and hearth, stone micro marble mantle	**2040**
Remove fireplace, brick up opening including air brick and vent	**220**
Remove chimney breast	**160**

COMMON ALTERATION WORKS
INTERIOR
Doors

	Number of Doors	£	RANGE	£
Doors				
Replace door, fix new ironmongery, decorate Flush door				
	1	**240**	to	**420**
	2	**380**	to	**740**
	5	**950**	to	**1850**
	8	**1520**	to	**2960**
Six panel door				
	1	**405**	to	**690**
	2	**710**	to	**1280**
	5	**1775**	to	**3200**
	8	**2840**	to	**5120**

	Cable Length to Existing (m)	Fittings (number)		
		1 £	2 £	5 £
New power sockets				
New surface mounted single socket outlet with PVCu conduit	1	84	115	205
	2	120	150	240
	5	160	190	280
New surface mounted double socket outlet with PVCu conduit	1	100	145	280
	2	135	180	315
	5	175	220	355
New flush mounted single socket outlet including cutting chase	1	92	130	235
	2	130	170	275
	5	170	210	315
New flush mounted double socket outlet including cutting chase	1	105	160	310
	2	145	200	350
	5	185	240	390
New light points				
New surface mounted ceiling rose, pendant and wall switch with PVCu conduit	4	155	200	335
	5	175	220	355
	6	195	240	375
New surface mounted ceiling lampholder and pull switch with PVCu conduit	1	105	135	225
	2	125	155	245
	5	180	210	300
New flush mounted ceiling rose, pendant and wall switch, cutting chase	4	140	185	320
	5	150	195	330
	6	160	205	340
New flush mounted ceiling lampholder and pull switch, cutting chase	1	95	125	215
	2	105	135	225
	5	135	165	255

	Suites £
New Sanitary suites	
Bathroom	
Basin and pressed steel bath	**1130**
Basin and plastic bath	**1260**
Low level cistern WC with seat, basin and pressed steel bath	**1720**
Low level cistern WC with seat, basin and plastic bath	**1850**
Shower Room	
Low level cistern WC with seat, basin and plastic shower tray	**1410**
Low level cistern WC with seat, basin and ceramic shower tray	**1530**
Cloakroom	
Low level cistern WC with seat and basin	**1010**
Kitchen	
Stainless steel sink with single bowl and drainer	**470**
Belfast sink	**580**

	RANGE		
	£		£
Replace heating system excluding pipework			
Wall mounted boiler, single and double panel radiators wall thermostat and programmer			
Clockwork programmer	**3620**	to	**5720**
Digital programmer	**4220**	to	**6320**
Replace heating system including pipework			
Wall mounted boiler, single and double panel radiators, pipework, wall thermostat and programmer			
Clockwork programmer	**5250**	to	**8610**
Digital programmer	**5850**	to	**9210**

	Length of Pipe Run (m)			
	5 £	10 £	15 £	20 £
Install new drain runs for new sanitary fittings				
100mm pipe				
Excavate through soft surface, average excavation depth 1000mm deep, replace pipe, make good ground	525	1000	1475	1950
Excavate through concrete or paving or tarmac surface, average excavation depth 1000mm deep, replace pipe, make good surface to match existing.	710	1435	2160	2885

	Single Items £
Form new manholes	
Excavate pit, concrete base, engineering brick sides, concrete cover slab with cast iron cover and frame, concrete benching and vitrified clay channel bends	
600 x 450 x 750mm deep internally	405
600 x 450 x 1000mm deep internally	525

2:6 TOTAL PROJECT COSTS

HOUSE EXTENSIONS

NOTE:
The works in this section generally **exclude** any
floor finishes.

Floor Size m	£	RANGE	£

HOUSE EXTENSIONS
Excludes forming openings to existing building

Single Storey with one window

	Floor Size m	£	RANGE	£
	3 x 3	**14000**	to	**17000**
	3 x 5	**17500**	to	**21500**
	4 x 4	**18500**	to	**23000**
	4 x 6	**24500**	to	**29500**
Two Storey with two windows				
	3 x 3	**23000**	to	**30000**
	3 x 5	**29000**	to	**36000**
	4 x 4	**31000**	to	**39000**
	4 x 6	**40000**	to	**50000**

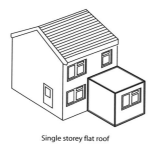

Single storey flat roof

Single storey pitched roof

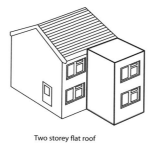

Two storey flat roof

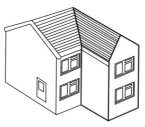

Two storey pitched roof

	Floor Size m	£	RANGE	£

CONSERVATORIES
Including radiator

	3 x 3	**8000**	to	**10000**
	4 x 4	**13000**	to	**17000**
	4 x 6	**19000**	to	**25000**

Including forming opening in existing external
cavity wall and new pair of glazed
doors, radiator

	3 x 3	**10000**	to	**12000**
	4 x 4	**15000**	to	**19000**
	4 x 6	**21000**	to	**27000**

GARDEN ROOMS
Similar to conservatories but with solid roof
Including radiator

	3 x 3	**8500**	to	**10500**
	4 x 4	**14000**	to	**18000**
	4 x 6	**20000**	to	**26000**

Including forming opening in existing external
cavity wall and new pair of glazed doors, radiator

	3 x 3	**10500**	to	**12500**
	4 x 4	**16000**	to	**20000**
	4 x 6	**22000**	to	**28000**

Floor Size m	£	RANGE	£

LOFT CONVERSIONS

Comprising clearing loft, relocating existing tanks, insulation, softwood framing and plasterboard to walls, insulation and plasterboard to ceiling, softwood floor, new straight flight staircase, new electrics and heating, openings in roof for windows.

		2 Windows £		4 Windows £
With Velux or similar windows				
	4 x 5	**13000**	to	**17000**
	6 x 5	**14000**	to	**18000**
	12 x 7	**21000**	to	**25000**
With dormer windows				
	4 x 5	**22000**	to	**36000**
	6 x 5	**23000**	to	**37000**
	12 x 7	**31000**	to	**44000**

Velux Windows

Dormer Windows

	RANGE		
	Floor Size		
	3 x 3m	3 x 5m	4 x 6m
	£	£	£

BASEMENT CONVERSIONS

Replace door and frame and staircase, plaster and paint walls and ceilings, screed floor, install skirting and decorate

6800	8000	9500

As above and including tanking walls and floor

15000	20000	24000

PORCHES

	750mm deep x		
	1200mm	1950mm	3000mm
	£	£	£

Canopies

Softwood frame and fascia, plywood soffit, plain tile roof, lead flashings, decoration

520	840	1340

GRP canopy with tile effect roof

340	440	670

	RANGE		
	Quality of Material		
	£		£

Enclosed porches

Purpose built PVCu on concrete base

2 x 1	2800	to	7000
3 x 2.5	4800	to	10000

Brick and timber or PVCu doors and windows

2 x 1	4500	to	6000
3 x 2.5	8500	to	10500

		RANGE		
		Quality of Materials		
		£		£
GARAGES				
Brick with flat roof				
Single width	6 x 3	**9500**	to	**15000**
Double width	6 x 5	**12500**	to	**20000**
Brick with pitched roof				
Single width	6 x 3	**10000**	to	**17000**
Double width	6 x 5	**13000**	to	**22000**
Purpose built, precast concrete				
Single width	5 x 3	**2600**	to	**4200**
Double width	5 x 5	**4200**	to	**7300**

		Without New Base £		With New Concrete Base £
CAR PORTS				
Installing on existing hardstanding or providing new concrete hardstanding				
Single width	2.6 x 3m	**1150**	to	**2000**
Double Width	4 x 3.5m	**2050**	to	**3700**
Cantilever canopy	2.4 x 3.2m	**2800**	to	**4500**

	RANGE	
	Quality of Materials	
	£	£

KITCHENS

Remove existing and install new units, fittings,
flooring, wall tiling and decoration

Size Range
> Terraced 8m^2 Detached 24m^2

Quality Range
> From: Standard DIY Superstore fittings and
> > vinyl floors
>
> To: Bespoke fittings and ceramic floor
> > tiling

TERRACED	**11000**	to	**25000**
DETACHED	**31000**	to	**120000**

BATHROOMS

Remove existing and install new sanitary fittings,
flooring, wall tiling and decoration

Size Range
> Terraced 6m^2 Detached 16m^2

Quality Range
> From: Standard DIY Superstore fittings and
> > vinyl floors
>
> To: Bespoke fittings and ceramic floor
> > tiling

TERRACED	**4100**	to	**10000**
DETACHED	**6200**	to	**40000**

PART 3

3:1 COSTING ASSUMPTIONS

Costs in this guide are for completing the work described as an individual job. They include contractors' overheads, scaffolding, where applicable, and VAT. They exclude any temporary works, contingencies and any fees that may be applicable.

The level of costs for the type of work envisaged by this guide are likely to be very sensitive to the context under which the work is procured, the quantity and complexity of the permanent work required and the degree of temporary works needed to achieve it.

The cost of building work is influenced by a wide range of factors, which vary with the individual circumstances of the client, the work, the location and the contractor. No two contractors are likely to charge exactly the same price for an item of work. The information in this guide can therefore only be a reasonable indication of the costs involved in carrying out the work described.

Material and component prices used in this guide are prices for small quantities without trade discounts. Discounts available on manufacturers' list prices will vary from supplier to supplier, and for different purchasers.

The prices contained within this guide are intended to apply to building modifications carried out generally within the United Kingdom (ie. they are based on a national average level). It will be recognised that price levels vary throughout the United Kingdom. In order to provide some guidance on regional pricing levels, the regional factors from the BCIS Study of Location Factors are reproduced in Part 3.3. The

Study of Location Factors is based on a survey of prices in new building schemes.

The items have been priced individually, that is, as if there was only one item of repair identified which required action, following a survey.

- The works as a whole will be carried out or managed by a small independent builder or specialist tradesman.
- One item of repair work will be carried out to a dwelling. Should more than one item of repair be necessary to a dwelling then there may be cost savings on the rates provided. For example, an elevation may require total repointing and the roof on that elevation may require reroofing. The scaffolding cost will therefore be reduced, as erecting and dismantling would be included in the guide in both rates.
- The modification work will be procured via some form of competitive process unless it is of a very specialist nature.
- A call out charge has been included in the rates where work is of a minor nature and labour time is less than a full or half day. This rate varies, depending upon the trade, and the appropriate figure is given in the 'Notes' at the bottom of the Table in which the call out rate applies.
- The modifications will be carried out in areas of the premises that can be isolated whilst work is carried out and to which contractors are allowed reasonably clear and unrestricted access.

- The work can be undertaken during normal construction industry working hours.
- Adequate and practical working space will be made available for the execution of the modifications and for the temporary storage of materials and items of equipment.
- Water and domestic power will be provided free of charge.

Although the above criteria set the basis of costs, the prices and estimates in the guide have been compiled to reflect the general nature of modification work, which tends to be small items of work of either a specialist or multi-trade nature, executed at disparate locations within existing premises, generally under less than ideal working conditions.

Savings in on-costs may be achieved where it is possible to arrange for more than one item of repair work to be programmed and undertaken as part of a single repair scheme.

Additional costs may occur in situations where work has to be carried out in areas of the premises which are constantly occupied and cannot be closed off from the occupants, or where operational use has to be preserved. Additional expense cost is also likely where specific constraints are imposed on the contractor such as restrictions on:

- Access
- Working space
- Storage of materials and equipment
- Removal of debris
- Hours of working
- Noise, dust, vibration
- Method of working, sequencing, phasing etc.

The degree of additional cost will depend on the severity of the constraints imposed and the user of the guide will need to assess their likely effect on both labour productivity and the temporary works needed (see also below) and adjust the estimate they are preparing accordingly.

The quantity and complexity of the modification work to be executed will be significant factors in the cost of the work.

It is likely, with the repair works envisaged by this guide, that materials and components will often be needed in small quantities. The benefits of economies of scale will therefore be experienced where work can be organised on a scale that allows materials to be purchased in larger volumes.

Where only a very small amount of permanent work is required at one location, its real cost per unit quantity may be significantly higher than it would be if a larger amount were needed. This is not just because the materials for small volumes of work have to be ordered at 'small quantity' prices but also because the relatively fixed labour costs in travelling to the location, preparation (setting out, positioning materials etc.) and final clearing away are still incurred and can significantly inflate the cost per unit quantity executed. For example, the price for replacing one light switch has included additional charges, as an electrician will be obliged to journey to the location to carry out work that will take a relatively small amount of time. There may be a minimum flat charge of say £50 or £75 for such work (referred to in some contexts as a 'call out charge'). On the other hand, if five or six light switches need to be repositioned then the impact of the 'call out charge' is lessened because it starts to be absorbed by the cost of the greater quantity of work that is required.

The work becomes more complex to carry out if it is in a difficult position (eg. working at heights or on upper floors) with restricted access and lack of working space or if it is of an exceptionally high standard or quality. The prices and estimates in this Guide generally allow for work which could be considered to be of average complexity only, with a range of prices being given in the tables, where relevant, to illustrate normal differences in specified standard or quality.

Where only small quantities of work are required, the fixed cost elements of any temporary works needed (dust screens, protective barriers etc.) can be a very significant part of the total cost of the work.

The prices and estimates in this guide do not include any allowances for temporary works, other than minor incidental supports and formwork where they are needed in excavation work, forming openings and concrete work. All other temporary work is considered as being part of 'preliminaries'. The exception to this is scaffolding, where costs, when stated, have been included in the Tables.

Additions of 20% on labour resource costs and 10% on material and plant resource costs have been made for Establishment Charges (office overheads) and Profit to all prices in

this Guide. The amounts these percentages generate are thought to be similar to those a prudent contractor would include to cover the costs of running a business and to allow for a reasonable profit.

An allowance of 12% has been made in the prices in this guide for Preliminaries (site overheads). Scaffolding, where required, has been priced additionally.

The extent of preliminaries will depend on the context of the job. They will vary widely according to the specific terms of the contract entered into as well as such criteria as the size, complexity and location of the project; the accessibility of the work; the amount of temporary works required; any restrictions imposed on working hours and practices; the feasibility and degree to which mechanical plant and equipment can be used; safety, health and welfare requirements.

No allowance has been made for Contingencies in the prices or estimates in this guide.

No allowance has been made in the prices and estimates within this guide for any Fees whatsoever.

Generally, the repairs, alterations and adaptations covered by this publication and which are contracted out are currently subject to VAT. All figures shown in the guide include VAT, at the current standard-rate of 17.5%.

The prices in this guide allow for work to be carried out during normal working hours. Extra cost will be incurred if work needs to be carried out in the evenings or at weekends.

The level of additional costs will vary depending on the working practices of the contractor but the nationally agreed overtime rates for building workers given below will give some indication.

Overtime	Basic Rates plus
Weekday or Saturday	
- First four hours	50%
- After first four hours	100%
Sunday	100%
Night Work (Permanent night working)	
Monday – Friday	25%
Weekends	100%

Where the term 'Prime Cost' (or its abbreviation 'PC') is used in this guide in relation to a material or component, the value it refers to represents the list price charged by the supplier excluding VAT, delivery charges and discounts. VAT has been added to the PC in the final rates shown in the Tables.

The prices in this guide have been compiled on the basis that normal levels of wastage will be experienced. However, it is possible with the class of work envisaged by this guide that some forms of direct waste would be more difficult to control. Also, a greater than normal amount of indirect waste may occur where only a very small quantity of a material or component is needed but it can only be supplied in standard can or pack sizes and charged accordingly.

It is probable that the debris and waste arising from the type of works envisaged by this guide will be left on site or disposed of by the contractor, dependent on the type of waste. For larger repair work, skips will be provided by the contractor and will be classified as active waste (containing organic material and matter such as paint and timber). Therefore, where items in the guide include for disposal (eg. demolitions and excavations), an allowance has been included for skip hire for the removal of active waste. In smaller items of replacement (eg. renewal of ironmongery, sanitary appliances and the like) disposal is deemed to be covered by overheads.

3:2 WHERE TO GET HELP –
USEFUL CONTACTS

1. Professional Bodies
The Royal Institution of Chartered Surveyors, 12 Great George Street, Parliament Square, London SW1P 3AD
Telephone: +44 (0)870 333 1600
Fax: +44 (0)20 7334 3811
E-mail: contactrics@rics.org
Web Site: http://www.rics.org/

RICS Find a Surveyor Service
To find a surveyor in your area visit the
Telephone: +44 (0)870 333 1600
Web Site: http://www.ricsfirms.com/
E-mail: contactrics@rics.org

The Royal Institute of British Architects, 66 Portland Place, London W1B 1AD
Telephone: +44 (0)906 302 0400
Fax: +44 (0)20 7255 1541
Web Site:
www.riba.org/go/RIBA/Home.html

The Institution of Structural Engineers, 11 Upper Belgrave Street, London SW1X 8BH
Telephone: +44 (0)20 7235 4535
Fax: +44 (0)20 7235 4294
Web Site:
http://.istructe.org.uk/

The Federation of Master Builders, Gordon Fisher House, 14-15 Great James Street,
London, WC1N 3DP
Telephone: +44 (0)20 7242 7583
Fax: +44 (0)20 7404 0296
E-mail: central@fmb.org.uk
Web Site: www.fmb.org.uk

2. Party Walls
The Royal Institution of Chartered Surveyors, 12 Great George Street, Parliament Square, London SW1P 3AD

RICS Party Wall Guidance –
Web site: http://www.rics.org/partywalls

RICS Party Walls Helpline –
Telephone: +44 (0)870 333 1600

The helpline will put you in touch with an experienced, local RICS surveyor who will provide you with up to 30 minutes free advice.

3. Contracts for Building Works
The Joint Contracts Tribunal Limited
Web site: www.jctltd.co.uk/ stylesheet.asp? file=492003233614
MW 98: Agreement for Minor Building Work
HG(A) 02: Agreement for Housing Grant Works

4. Book Shops

RIBA Bookshops

Telephone: +44 (0)20 7496 8394
Fax: +44 (0)20 7374 8500
Email: jct@ribabooks.com

RICS Books

Tel: +44 (0)870 333 1600
(press option 3)
Fax: +44 (0)20 7334 3851
Email: mailorder@rics.org
Website: http://www.ricsbooks.com

CIP Limited

Telephone: +44 (0)870 078 4400
Fax: +44 (0)870 078 4401
Email: sales@cip-books.com

5. Builders Federation

The National Federation of Builders
National Office, 55 Tufton Street,
London, SW1P 3QL

Telephone: +44 (0)870 8989 091
Fax: +44 (0)870 8989 096
Email: national@builders.org.uk
Web site: http://www.builders.
org.uk/nfb/

6. Trade Federations

Painters & Decorators
Painting & Decorating Association,
Head Office, 32 Coton Road, Nuneaton,
Warwickshire CV11 5TW

Telephone: 024 7635 3776
Fax: 024 7635 4513
Web site:
http://www.paintingdecoratingassociati
on.co.uk/

Electrical Contractors
The Electrical Contractors' Association
(ECA)
ECA Head Office
ESCA House, 34 Palace Court, London,
W2 4HY

Telephone: +44 (0)20 7313 4800
Fax: +44 (0)20 7221 7344
Web site: http://www.eca.co.uk/

3:3 LOCATION FACTORS

The prices in this guide are average UK prices. The map overleaf shows regional pricing factors which indicate the general variability of pricing levels around the country. The factors are taken from the BCIS Study of Location Factors.

Adjusting for Location

The following examples show how to adjust the prices for a 3 x 3m single storey extension with one window.

Single storey extension as Page 172   **£17000**

	Factor	£
Scotland	0.99	**16830**
North West	0.96	**16320**
North	0.99	**16830**
Yorkshire & Humberside	1.00	**17000**
East Midlands	0.93	**15810**
West Midlands	0.96	**16320**
Wales	0.91	**15470**
East Anglia	1.01	**17170**
South East	1.06	**18020**
Greater London	1.12	**19040**
South West	0.99	**16830**
Northern Ireland	0.67	**11390**

Scotland
0.99

N.Ireland
0.67

North
0.99

Yorkshire &
Humberside
1.00

North
West
0.96

East Midlands
0.93

West Midlands
0.96

East Anglia
1.01

Wales
0.91

GL
1.12

South West
0.99

South East
1.06

3:4 INFLATION INDICES

The costs in this guide have been priced at fourth quarter 2005 price level.

The table below provides percentage adjustments on the costs of the estimated work from the price level in the guide to when the work is anticipated to be carried out on site.

Percentages figures all updated from 4Q05		Percentage update
Quarter		
4Q06	(October, November, December)	1.045
1Q07	(January, February, March)	1.053
2Q07	(April, May, June)	1.061
3Q07	(July, August, September)	1.077
4Q07	(October, November, December)	1.081
1Q08	(January, February, March)	1.085
2Q08	(April, May, June)	1.098
3Q08	(July, August, September)	1.122
4Q08	(October, November, December)	1.126
1Q09	(January, February, March)	1.130
2Q09	(April, May, June)	1.142
3Q09	(July, August, September)	1.163
4Q09	(October, November, December)	1.167

Adjusting for Inflation

The following examples show how to adjust the prices for a 3 x 3m single storey extension with one window.

Single storey extension as Page 172   **£17000**

Estimated date construction:	Inflation percentage		Revised Project Cost
November 2006	(4Q06)	1.045	£17760
March 2007	(1Q07)	1.053	£17900
September 2008	(3Q08)	1.122	£19080

3:5 HOUSE TYPES

The following diagrams have been produced to indicate the types of houses used in the production of various tables in the guide which give costs for whole house, elevations, floors, rooms etc.

Terraced House

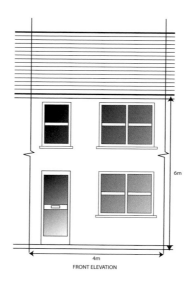

6m

4m

FRONT ELEVATION

Detached House

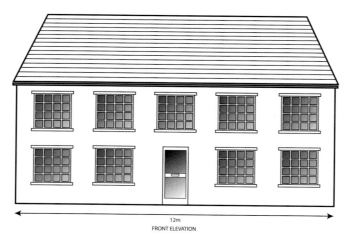

12m

FRONT ELEVATION

GLOSSARY

Architraves – timber moulding around door and window openings.

Battens – Wood strips onto which something is fitted. *For example:* roof tiles.

Beads – A small moulding covering a join.

Blown or Live Plaster – Plaster which has come away from the wall having lost its bond.

Brick Bond – The arrangement of bricks built to ensure the walls stability. *For example:* stretcher bond, Flemish bond.

Cavity Wall – The outside wall of the property, made up of an inner and outer layer or 'skin' with a void (cavity) between, often filled with insulation.

Contingencies or Contingency Sum – A sum of money allowed in your budget, on top of the agreed quote from the contractor, to allow for unforeseen works. An amount, either expressed as a percentage of the work or a lump sum. This will be for work that has not been included in the specification or shown on the drawings, but it may be advisable to allow a figure in case unknown items are encountered.
For example: The works may include replacing some floorboards. However when the old boards are removed, the joists supporting may be rotten and require replacing. The contractor will not be aware, until the boards are lifted, that the joists are rotten, and he will therefore not have included a sum in his quote to cover this work.

Coping – A protective capping at the top of a wall. *For example:* precast concrete coping.

Dpc, 'Damp Proof Course' – An impervious membrane built into brickwork to prevent movement of water through the brickwork. *For example:* laid about two brick courses above the ground, around window and door openings, made of hessian based bitumen felt, slate, etc.

Distribution Board – A unit containing switches, circuit breakers, fuses etc, which protect the electrical circuits in a property.

Eaves - An overhang of the roof beyond the wall below.

Estimate – An approximate price for one part or all of the work. This is sometimes used to mean quotation (see Page 193).

Fanlight – A window over an internal door to provide natural light into the corridor.

Flashing – A metal sheet used to deflect water and prevent ingress. *For example:* at the junction between the roof and wall

Flaunching – A cement mortar fillet at the top of a chimney stack, around the pots.

Flush Door – A door that has completely flat faces.

Foundations – A concrete or brick construction under walls, which provides support to those walls and structure above.

Gable – The upper part of an outer wall at the end of a pitched roof.

Grout – A material that fills the joints in wall and floor tiles and helps to prevent water ingress.

Hardcore – This is a material of broken bricks etc, which is laid under concrete beds or in soakaways.

Header Tank – A small open cistern (tank) that feeds water to a central heating system.

Herringbone Strutting – A zigzag pattern of timber that is fixed between joists to provide additional support.

Hip – The line adjoining parts of a pitched roof at the external angle of a building.

Hip Tile – A shaped roof tile which covers the hip.

Hipped Roof – A pitched roof whose ends are also pitched.

Insitu – Work which is constructed on site rather than constructed off site and brought into the works.

Ironmongery – Fittings installed to doors and windows to allow them to operate. *For example:* locks, bolts.

Joist – A support for floor and ceiling.

Knotting – A varnish to stabilise knots in wood.

Location Factors –Prices for work vary from region to region. The prices in this book are average UK prices and adjustments should be made on estimates for the location of the work.

Lintel – Concrete, steel or timber beam over an opening to support a wall above.

Making Good – The finishing touches that bring work up to scratch.

Manholes – A construction of brick, concrete or pvc that is situated in the ground where down pipes enter the underground drainage system or where there is a bend or junction in the underground system. The manhole will have a removable cover and the pipe will be open in order that inspections can be made.

Mullion – A vertical post in a window, dividing the window into parts.

Newel – Vertical post at the top and bottom of a staircase.

Nosing – The rounded end to stair tread. This projects beyond the riser.

Pantile - A curved 's' shaped or 'u' shaped roof tile.

PC Sum (Prime Cost Sum) – A sum of money allowed for an item of work or materials supplied by the client. *For example:* installation of a fire alarm system by a specialist already selected by the client, or the cost of a bathroom suite to be purchased by the client.

Pebble Dash – Wall finish with stones bedded in a rendered external wall.

Pitch – The slope of a roof.

Plain Tile – A flat rectangular roof tile.

Plasterboard – Prefabricated sheets of plaster, which are used for walls and ceilings.

Prefabricated – An item of the works made off site and brought onto the site. *For example:* roof truss.

Preliminaries – These are costs for items that are required to carry out the contract other than the actual construction costs. *For example:* travelling costs, the hire of scaffolding or other items of plant (e.g. cement mixers), office and other administrative charges.

Provisional Sum – An amount included in the contract sum/agreed quote for additional works that are not fully specified. *For example:* fitted units to a bedroom are required but the design/materials are not finalised at the time the contract is agreed. By inserting a reasonable sum, the contractor can allow for his overheads and include these works into his programme.

Purlin – A horizontal beam part of the way up the rafters. This helps to prevent the roof sagging.

Quote/Quotation – The price offered by the contractor to do the work.

Rafters – Roof timbers that rise from the eaves to the ridge to support a pitched roof.

Render – A coating of cement and sand applied to the face of an external wall.

Retention – A sum of money set aside by the client (you) from the contract sum until the works are completed to your satisfaction.

Ridge – The top apex of a pitched roof.

Ridge Tile – A tile, commonly half round, which is laid along the ridge, bedded in cement mortar.

Ring Main – The power circuit for electrical sockets in the property.

Riser (to stairs) – The upright part of a stair between treads.

Riser (water) – The vertical water pipe from the mains.

Rising Damp – Water that has come from below ground and rises up through the masonry by capillary action.

Roof Truss – A prefabricated structural timber framework to support the roof.

RSJ – 'Rolled steel joist'. A steel beam.

Sarking Felt – A waterproof felt under the roof tile battens.

Screed – A layer of fine concrete, which is used to provide a smooth surface prior to laying a floor finish.

Septic tank – An underground chamber, which collects the foul water from the property via waste and drain pipes.

Sill – The bottom horizontal member of a door or window frame.

Skim – The thin finishing coat of plaster that provides a smooth finish for decoration etc.

Soakaways – An excavated hole filled with hardcore to collect the rainwater from roofs taken through drain pipes into this pit.

Stack – The vertical pipe that carries waste water from toilets, baths, sinks etc to the drainage system.

String – The sloping board that carries the treads and risers of a staircase.

T & G boarding – T & G or tongued and grooved boarding is the traditional softwood flooring construction when the boards are jointed together.

Trap – A curved section of drain that holds water and provides a seal that prevents any odours returning into the room.

Tread – The horizontal part of a tread that is used to walk up and down the staircase.

TRV – Thermostatic radiator valve. This valve regulates the temperature of the radiator.

Underpinning – A method of supporting the existing external walls by excavating under the existing foundations and providing additional foundations.

Variations – These are work items that arise during the construction that were not allowed for in the quote. *For example:* during replacement of some floor boards, the joists below are found to be rotten. The quote only allowed for replacing the boards, the replacement of the joists is therefore a variation.

Verge – The edge of the pitched roof at the end of the property with a gable. The verge runs from the eaves to the ridge.

Verge Tile – The tiles at the end of the roof, running from the eaves to the ridge. These tiles are bedded in cement mortar.

INDEX